Please Don't Kill the Freshman

PLEASE, DON'T KILL THE FRESH-MAN

a memoir
by: ZOE TROPE

HarperTempest
An Imprint of HarperCollinsPublishers

For information address HarperCollins Children's Books, a division
of HarperCollins Publishers, 1350 Avenue of the Americas,
New York, NY 10019.

Library of Congress Cataloging-in-Publication Data
Trope, Zoe.
    Please don't kill the freshman / Zoe Trope.
       p. cm.
    Summary: A memoir of the then-fifteen-year-old author's high school
experience to that point, in which diary entries reflect her struggles, angst,
and rebellion.
    ISBN 0-06-052936-9—ISBN 0-06-052937-7 (lib. bdg.)
    ISBN 0-06-052938-5 (pbk.)
    1. Trope, Zoe—Diaries. 2. High school students—United States—
Biography. [1. Trope, Zoe. 2. Diaries. 3. Youths' writings.] I. Title.
CT275.T8755A3 2003   2003004411
305.235'092—dc21

Typography by Alison Donalty
❖
First HarperTempest paperback edition, 2004

Parts of this work were previously published in different form by
Future Tense Press, 2001.

Visit us on the World Wide Web!
www.harpertempest.com

For my parents:
This is all your fault.

"We rarely forget events that cause us to feel this way."
—Frank B. McMahon et al., *Psychology and You*

LIST OF CHARACTERS

linux shoe—fourteen years old. freshman. best friend. homosexual. beautiful. has made me cry many, many times. disgustingly insightful. plays cello. reads philosophy. asked me why Tosca had to die.

plum sweater—eighteen years old. senior. of the literary persuasion. very dry laugh. very soft (muddy brown) hair.

wonka boy—fifteen years old. freshman. very *fifteen*. listens to angry music. thinks his parents are out to make his life a living hell. whines. needs someone. has completely random moments of blue-eyed beauty.

braid bitch—fifteen years old. freshman. a girl with very long brown hair. Case Boy's temporary girlfriend. smiles to murder the people she loves. fucks with her teeth wide open. spreads rumors. a typical nine-year-old mentality (she said he said I told you so!).

case boy—fifteen years old. freshman. quiet in his own repressed way. listens to angry music. likes anime, guinea pigs, and the Metallica t-shirt I gave him for his birthday.

also prone to expressing his violence through video games.

techno boy—seventeen years old. junior. has a red car. works at a restaurant. it hurts when he smiles. dandruff. computers, electronic music. seeking a girl that won't eat his heart with a steak knife.

fishsticks—English teacher with rectangular glasses. also known as the blond Beck wanna-be. listens to Radiohead and talks with his hands.

cherry bitch—most beautiful girl ever. sixteen years old. sophomore. wears juicy red lipstick. smokes cigarettes like she wants to fuck them with her bright red mouth. makes art with her hands. makes sounds with her hands. makes beauty with her hands.

jar guard —English teacher who is far too nice. too young to be burned out yet. listens to U2. enjoys the occasional back rub. has a wife. lets anyone write anything on the dry erase board in his classroom.

greasy buddy holly—self-descriptive. tortoiseshell glasses. I'm rather envious of his occupation. thirty-something. I could say more but he would cut off my lips.

vegan grrl—seventeen years old. senior. literally a genius. wants to save the planet. eats a lot of fruit. has thin lips and yellow hands. is good at: playing music (flute, guitar, piano, etc.), singing, physics, poetry, art, chemistry, calculus, and saving small children from Ecuador. can't save herself.

curry—fifteen years old. freshman. mother is literally insane. very conservative family. he likes dressing up in women's clothing (watched *Rocky Horror* too many times). also enjoys listening to bad punk rock music and hating society.

raskolnikov—twenty-seven years old. radical goatee. wants revolution like small children beg for candy in the checkout line at a grocery store. hands shake a lot. drinks iced coffee. molds my brain. commie. brilliant. moves in very calculated ways. dresses in black. oh yes, you heard me, he dresses in black.

sloppy charcoal—ex-girlfriend of Techno Boy. during certain portions of my life, they were going out. she's one of those overly aggressive obnoxious little bitches who knows absolutely everything about everything and *knows* they know everything about everything.

midwestern tackiness—extremely neurotic French teacher. you know that one teacher you had in high school who was an utter bitch no matter what you did? yeah, well, she's it.

trois.douze
"The amendment that protects . . ." Sharp voice falling on muffled ears. I got a perfect score, plus five extra credit points. Pardon me for not seeing the point of listening. I could be doing something constructive or even listening but I choose not to. It has never been clarified if apathy is by choice or due to environmental factors. I choose apathy, then regret it later. Roll around frustratedly on my bed and fret about the things I should've done . . . When I woke up, it felt wrong. The random objects cluttering my room were illuminated by a disgustingly bright gray light. I sit up and look out the window. The streets are dry and quiet and the bland oatmeal sky stretches out over the houses without deviation or ending. I want nothing more than to crawl back into my marijuana nightmares but I decide against it. "Write the total over points possible. . . ." He's still talking. I'm pondering the paper cut on my knuckle. This is not an education. I am in day care.

✦✦

Houston, we've lost power. The clocks have stopped. Buzzing of fluorescent radiation ceased. Hustled voices continue to bounce and break. Tapping of a pencil, silent ink moving over bleached paper. Why couldn't I at least be stuck in a class with people I can stand?

trois.treize
Yesterday, in the library, he was there with his marmalade hat and docile tongue. Librarians itch and curl their hair tighter. "Are you looking for poetry? That isn't poetry." Bitch. Do not tell me what art is and isn't. And stop looking over my fucking shoulder like I'm a criminal when I'm on the internet. You're the one who got stuck working in a high school library. No one chooses that profession, I'm sure.

The literary magazine: weekly orgy of delivered pizza, liter bottles of soda, alterna-teens, loser geeks, art-poetry submissions. We eat and laugh too loud. We make gagging noises at love poetry. We put our elitist words in a book that is published in the spring. The administration does not like us. The administration does not like me because my poem, featuring the word *faggot*, was published in the winter 'zine.

Today's meeting makes me think in four-letter words. My muddy-haired girl stolen by charcoal freckles. Vegan

Grrl's muscles kneading my own into submission. Dark denim overalls inspected by my hands. Plum Sweater tickled and squealing. Arms unwilling to unhinge. Lips mouthing unwanted words.

trois.quatorze

Wise to listen, not to speak. Stupid forecasting ruining my plans yet again. Irony tastes like lead water. I avoid it. Greek roots fail to teach me new words. He said, Iconoclastic. He asked for an example. I said, Sinéad O'Connor. No one else knew what I was talking about. That's fine.

I read teen magazines when I was younger. Why are they called teen magazines if girls start reading them when they're ten? They are mainly devoted to fashion. One reader wrote in, "I never wear the same outfit twice!" 5,214 outfits. Worn fingers of Indian girls. Frizzy black hair. Clicking tongues and wrinkled knuckles. My age but much too old. All so this girl can wear 5,214 outfits. How many pairs of jeans have her fingers sewn? Too many. I wish I remembered where the reader lived. I would've sent her to Haiti or India or Indonesia, where she could have sewn all 5,214 of her own goddamn outfits.

I like sour things. Sour gummi bears. Warheads. Lemons. Things like that. The idea that I am sour is not an insult. Perhaps a compliment. Would I really be unhappy to be put inside someone's mouth, swished around, feel the puckering of someone's cheeks? Would it be so terrible to give someone pain to give them pleasure? I am a masochistic candy cane, lick 'em lolly, and gummi girl all in one. The pain you seek is me. Just me.

trois.quinze

Unsure where to draw the line between the figments on my shoulders. Ever-convincing devil toying with me. Angel reading a magazine, paying no attention. So bored. The computer programming teacher was gone again. Server down again. Substitute apathetic, again. I open my mouth and breathe words on Techno Boy. McDonald's? Hmm. Money? Flash my cheap wallet at him with crumpled bills inside. Okay. Library pass. Grab it. Run. The class waved at us as we got into the car. Mmm, lead water. McDonald's tasted better. He drove me home. Nice. Even if his girlfriend is a Sloppy Charcoal bitch. I scare my mother and she doesn't even bother to chastise me. Although I thought the substitute saw us, apparently he did not. Lesson learned for today? You can lie to a substitute, skip class, have numerous eyewitnesses, and even tell your parents that you skipped—and still receive no punishment whatsoever.

Interpersonal relationships learned about in health class. So disinterested in hearing about this girl fuck a senior and trying to shove her tongue into his heart. What a whore. I'm sure others would say the same about her. Not me. I am just a lemon with little more to offer than puckered cheeks. One day I can be an apple. One day I'll learn how to be sweet.

trois.dix-sept
Blond Beck wanna-be (Fishsticks, we'll call him) calmly explaining id, ego, superego. Shut up. Apathetic brunette giggling disinterested in your college theories. I would love him if he weren't a fakephonyliar. Yuck. Lead water. Classmates trying to convince me of the themes of Huck Finn. I know I'm intelligent. I hear it constantly. The fact that I despise this classic work of fiction (and will most likely fail the final exam) greatly disturbs me. Why do I need Fishsticks-wanna-be-Beck-groove-loving-guitar-playing-trying-to-be-young-and-hip's approval? Because I'm still weak and petty. And I need to hear good words to make everything all right. Clench my teeth and force myself not to whine.

I got my new *Mother Jones* yesterday. The only fourteen-year-old who can read political magazines. Better yet, who chooses to read political magazines. I can hear my brother's voice reminding me to stop being so fucking serious. I don't know why caring makes me a serious person. I eat meat. I get B's on my progress report. I forget my homework. It has taken far too long, but I've learned to accept these simple truths. I'll be absolutely fine as long as I just don't get a B on my actual report card. The number 4.0 is calm, comforting. If you'll excuse me, I need to go breathe into a paper bag and take some quiet pink pills. I can make things right again.

trois.dix-huit

Today's assembly was a mockery of my strength. They have none, only a lack of dignity which allows them to make fools of themselves publicly. Too much to ask for them to play OUR music as they filed into the gym. Too much to ask that they stop talking for FIVE seconds while we try to. Microphones are useless. School assemblies, even when I'm a part of them, are nauseating. They are vegetables; they should throw themselves at us. We tried. It was a multimedia presentation of guilt tactics. "Recycle or Die" would have been a better slogan. I am such a loser geek. I'd burn this earth club t-shirt but I'm too lazy. And the toxins from the smoke would pollute the air.

Greasy Buddy Holly proposed even more than plane crashes. I try to remember to breathe. . . . Words are scarce, dreams are many. Blond curls in blue VW bug flipping over and over, unable to drive. Can't handle control. I pray not to die. Pippi Longstocking is a bitch. So is trying to be her. So is filming a video for English class. Head sore from wire hangers. That was only Saturday.

trois.vingt

45 minutes wasted in the counseling office. Please explain to me why everything moves so goddamn slowly. And why the counselors care so little.

In French, we watched a video about Vincent van Gogh. Midwestern Tackiness displayed through badly curled hair. "You need to watch this. It's culture." Fuck culture. Could you teach the language? Or, better yet, actually go to the country and hear the fucking language? Mad cow blabbering incessantly. Thank God I won't have to take this class next year.

Thin vegan lips explain excitedly, "Tre Arrow called me last night." I die of envy. I saw him at the earth club conference in the fall. What a God. A Vegan Adonis. The man lived on a ledge and crapped in a bucket! He should be revered, acknowledged, worshiped! Or, according to the assistant vice principal, he should bathe.

trois.vingt-et-un

I pity the pretty little Mormon girls. Their mouths always curl up in disgust when they walk past me. The thought bubble above their head reads, "My dear lord! What a heathen!" Bitch. A conservative Baptist with big feet asks Wonka Boy, *(hushed, embarrassed plead)* "What'sanorgasm?" I cackle delightedly. Who will be the real heathen when her forty-eight-year-old pastor knocks her up? I must stop being so cynical. I know far too many angry twenty-somethings who got burned out in high school. Hanging out with these witty sarcastic vile twenty-somethings really helps me. I like them. My parents, however, do not. To them I am pleading with the raincoat men to come and rape me. I am trying not to drown. I am trying to bloom. Please don't kill the flowers.

trois.vingt-quatre

My biology teacher is trying to give a review lecture for the test on Friday. I could get a zero on the test and still have an A in the class. It's kind of depressing. I think my time is spent much more productively by writing, glaring at her, sipping orange juice, and nibbling on cheerios. I am not an elitist. I am just a cheerio junkie. I wish I had my *Mother Jones*. It's easier to read and drown out her voice.

Rejected by the Plum Sweater and muddy brown hair. Loved and then rejected. Chastised and then stroked. STOP ABUSING ME!!! Oh, but I want more. Please don't stop. No! No more dihybrid crosses or punnett squares or sex-linked double-allele chromatic heterozygous codominant genotypic ratios! I'm going to start drooling like the rest of my classmates. And then, after that, she'll break out the safety crayons and we can have art time. Orange juice and honey nut cheerios are a delicacy. I had to argue with my science teacher last year to get into this class and now I sit here with these morons who don't give a fuck. Argh. I will not be an angry twenty-something. I will not grow into an angry twenty-something. I will not . . . meet. my. fate.

trois.vingt-sept

Plum Sweater on my voice mail. Heart palpitations induced. What a nerdy goddess. I'm going to faint. My fingers are shaking. I can't decide whether to squeal excitedly with a friend or call her back. I decide to call her. We laugh. Our voices are fake. She sounds so young. Painting pottery tomorrow? Great. Okay. I'll call you when I get home. I can't get over it. Is it a date? Is she interested in me? I'm so fucked up. I am SOOO . . . fourteen. I can't stop shaking. She said she finds me "interesting." My heart is pounding. I can't believe this. It's Plum Sweater.

trois.vingt-huit

Fucking Plum Sweater. What a bitch. She has company, church, cleaning, *The West Wing*. After more than twenty-four hours of a girlscout–knotted stomach and shaking hands, I am told I have to wait until Saturday. I'm going to wring her neck after I hold her forever. My fingers click idly. I find this boy I know and ask him to come over. I tell him I can't be alone. My shiny Linux Shoe agrees and scurries. We eat toasted cheese sandwiches and I rub my nose into his 100% cotton trousers. Such a marvelous fag. He tells me about making love on fresh-cut grass. I want to cry. I'm supposed to be hugging a Plum Sweater. These gray trousers will have to do.

trois.vingt-neuf

Linux Shoe and I attempt to learn, even though it's our spring break. We go to a pseudo-hip bookstore in the middle of suburbia and browse homosexual literature. He defines boys by their height and weight, similar to coffee drinks. Venti dark roasts and grande tiger mochas. I'm sipping hot chocolate and he's burning his lips on chai tea. The tea ends up in his lap anyway, thanks to my shaky hands. This was only Thursday.

trois.trente

Forced out of slumber to argue with my hair. I claim defeat and face day three with my Linux Shoe. He is appreciative for his cardboard poetry magnets and faggot anthology. We stuff ourselves with homemade Mexican food and brown bottled cream soda. I'm ecstatic to not be alone.

I don't understand girls who—wait, never mind, I just don't understand girls. Especially the ones who smear their faces with brightly colored crap every chance they get. I want to shove that lipstick pencil into her eye. Oh, the people you can judge while riding public transportation. We return home to my bed and our bad music. We listen to muses this time, angry horny anti-Catholic ones with names like Paula and Tori. He smiles. I cling to my Linux Shoe and rub my head into his belly and smell his clean blue shirt. He was always the clean one. My digital clock ticks. I am left alone in my empty double bed.

trois.trente-et-un

I take a shower and sigh. I am not looking forward to Plum Sweater, amazingly. We chase each other through the phone lines. Eventually, 2:45. I get as little work done on my eight-minute speech as possible. We lazily paint pottery. She tells me about choosing a school, her best friend's competitiveness, birth control, her mother walking in on her when she was having sex. I feel like she could drown me in a spoonful of water or crush me with her fingernail clippings. I realize I have no chance.

quatre.deux

Linux Shoe was choke-sobbing this morning. His parents removed the modem cord from his vein. No more instant messaging and e-mail attachments and online diary poetry updates. She forces her Midwestern Tackiness down our throats and I laugh. The woman is insane and can't dress to save her life. She wears the sort of t-shirts you pick up on vacation as souvenirs. Plum Sweater at her locker. I pause briefly to toy with her hair and she smiles. The boy with the giant black case (Case Boy, even) returns home from Alaska. He gives his Braid Bitch a stuffed moose with a painful smile. I can't wait to cut off all her hair when she breaks his heart.

My Linux Shoe gives me a poem in black ink. I lovingly shove it in my black backpack. Teacher gives us forty-five minutes to fill in a worksheet. I sigh aimlessly and scribble, waiting to run to English class where I can do nothing.

quatre.trois

My Linux Shoe's current crush is telling me about hepatitis. I like his long smooth neck and think he would look good with Linux Shoe. How adorable. He has shaky hands that shuffle his note cards weakly. I think of Linux Shoe's wish to kiss callused fingertips. Damn him for being him. I'll just keep lusting vicariously through Linux.

So exhausted. Four hours in a smoke-filled pool hall that I did not want to be in. How many times did I explain to the Case Boy that I did not want to go? He pulls in to the driveway the same time as my mother and I (we have finished our tedious errands and have not yet stepped out of the car). "Come on, you're going." I grind my teeth silently and humiliate myself, hitting balls clumsily with an over-size stick. Case Boy reminds me to stop whining and being such a bitch and I should be glad to get out of the house and not sitting on my fat ass in front of the computer. He has not touched me but I feel like I've been slapped. I grimace and shut my mouth. I feel like a fool and my desire for my Linux Shoe grows stronger (we spent the greater part of fourth period pointing at boys, giggling, and making erotic statements). When I leave the pool hall, tired and considerably more humble, Case Boy escorts me out and gives me the most disgusting hateful smile when I tell him I won't be coming back.

quatre.quatre

I promise myself I'm going to laugh about this someday. My dreams are obscure and frightening but I refuse to leave them. Linux Shoe greets me in the hallway. We pace to the choir room and gnaw on our cuticles. I shuffle to the classroom of France and Midwestern Tackiness. I ask her if I can turn something in and she tells me not to be rude. I promise myself I'm going to laugh about this someday. . . . Elijah Wood can't act. His portrayal of Huck Finn makes me want to vomit. My Linux Shoe sits by me at lunch in his classic black jacket. I squeeze his blue jean–covered knee and hate the Case Boy for trying to tell me that Linux Shoe will not find anyone. To quote Wonka Boy: "LYING BITCH." He is right. So right. I can't wait to program a computer and get yelled at by a boring ex-hippie (a substitute, obviously) . . . Linux Shoe follows me home and into my bed. We waste time, drinking too much, holding each other. We finally give up and walk around the neighborhood, softly revealing secrets to each other in the clean quiet of the evening. Fresh-cut grass is everywhere. We laugh. We sip cold water and continue to giggle. I try, so hard, not to cry when he leaves.

quatre.neuf

My weekend almost completely devoid of Linux Shoe. He wanders into the library and flops onto a wooden chair. I peel the black headphones off his head and hug him around his shoulders. We miss a beautiful pizza, poetry, Braid Bitch's birthday party. We bite our lips so hard they bleed when teenage pseudo-elitists dressed in sophisticated black turtlenecks read political magazines. We desire their shoulder blades, arms, and waists. My lip hurts. The sun falls into the earth and I walk with the Wonka Boy. He bounces on an invisible pogo stick, explaining and describing his first game of spin the bottle. I nod and try not to smirk (FAILURE). I chew my raw fingernails, waiting to touch my Linux Shoe.

quatre.dix

I love her Midwestern Tackiness. I've learned to giggle when she screams, read my book of patriarchal theories when she tells me to study, and I refuse to rat on anyone who flips her off. It's just hilarious. I move into a political class next and ignore the teacher. Three tests on Thursday. My grade is going to rhyme with fuck. . . . My neck throbs. Fucking state tests. Neck bent over fill-in-the-bubble hell. I feel sick to my stomach. Maybe because Linux Shoe was not at lunch or because I have no more clear packaging tape left. Oh my dear and undying love of adhesive. What would my locker look like without you? It would be a tragedy. I'm starving, but I don't want food.

quatre.onze
Linux Shoe whines loudly about his inability to write, lack of a boyfriend, overinterest in the straight boys. I sigh and hit his cheek with the back of my hand. He honestly believes that if he does not have a boyfriend before he turns fifteen, his entire life will be over. No reason to live. No will to go on. Because, so far, this is his entire life. And he's gone his entire life without a boyfriend. I laugh and shake my head. When he sits still, he wears a cloak of longing that presses down on his shoulders, pushing him into the ground, weighing down the corners of his mouth. I keep my mouth closed, because if I opened it, tears would come out. Some beautiful man is going to steal him away from me someday. Too soon. Far, far too soon.

quatre.douze
Yesterday I learned all my friends are gay and I feel responsible. Wonka Boy, the boy with black hair, exploring his

uncertainty as I sip Sprite. I hold him, filled with guilt. Not a bad score. Out of four male friends, I've managed to turn 2.5 gay. Beat that, Margaret Cho. In an hour I'll be in English class, flunking my Fuck Finn—er, Huck Finn test. I'll be listening to Wonka Boy and Case Boy argue, and Case Boy will devalue my humanity. Cherry Bitch, my insomniac, pries secrets from tired cold fingers and I click for her like a happy dance. Just one of those insane rich messed-up beat hippie-chick bitch art girls—fucking Cherry Bitch. Plum Sweater looked zombielike this morning and I made desperate attempts to console her (failure as usual). I stayed up far too late with my Cherry Bitch and my eyes are raw and sore. Sleep.

quatre.treize

Suffering through bad luck. Yesterday I took the MetroAreaExpress (MAX) to a place of communal teenagerism (malls make me itch). Wonka Boy admits his homosexuality over a giant slice of pizza. We buy gifts for the Case Boy (a Metallica t-shirt and a cheetah-print fez). Case Boy will be ungrateful (expected).

quatre.quinze

My Linux Shoe and I waste away the last few hours of the weekend. We shove M&M's into our mouths hungrily, walk, hold each other. Earlier he visited me at the library. Easter Sunday, so the place was packed with emptiness and silence, except for a cello, a flute, and a cute boy making free coffee. Curry sucked down three mochas and a black tiger. He frightens me. I come home and wait for my Linux Shoe, resisting Monday like a fussy baby who presses her lips together and refuses to eat applesauce. This was only Sunday.

quatre.seize

Monday. Now. Today. Welcome to Career Week. Please shoot me. Please. Please. Stuck in one classroom for an entire fucking week. What have I accomplished today? We arrive, play overused get-to-know-you games, and then he lets us out to wander the halls. I feel lost. Returning, we make collages, read worksheets, and fill out surveys that will tell us what to be when we "grow up." I know I'm in kindergarten because we can't leave the room unless we have our laminated name tags on blue yarn. Cherry Bitch jerks clumsily in a silver shopping cart, running up and down the hallway. She manages to pick yellow weeds and tape them to my locker with a note: "'heart' the Cherry Bitch." I pluck one of the yellow weeds blooming on my locker and twirl it between my fingers. I hand it to a girl whose name I don't know, but she wears a pentagram neck-lace, too. She just smiles and thanks me. It is good to remember that not everything is hate. . . . I'm just sitting here now, staring at the clock, loathing nonproductivity and the twangy country music radio station he insists on playing. This girl behind me is whining and blubbering about her ex-boyfriend. I resist the urge to slap her as hard as I can. I don't hate my peers, simply because it's a waste of time. I can, however, dislike my teachers who breed and favor these apathetic products of noneducation. I've wasted six hours here. I could be at the library or in a park or visiting a museum or ANYWHERE but I'm here. I hate school because it is so traditional and accepted and so normal. What college would take me without a high school diploma? Good colleges, traditional colleges, would not. Sometimes I acknowledge it is not the fault of the school. It's my own fault for being so unmotivated and ready to blame. I see these things but do not react. Four days until the beach. Forty-five minutes until I can leave. I must keep breathing until then. I'm tempted to just pass out. It would be grand. It would be art. Would anyone notice?

quatre.dix-sept
Fuck. All I can say about today. Cherry Bitch grins lopsidedly and gives me little yellow pills: vivarin. I fill out more career-grown-up worksheets and then scurry to the bathroom in my fuzzy blue slippers and cup my hand under the dirty faucet, holding water on my tongue and swallowing down the pretty little pill. I hate pills. Swallow down another one during lunch with 100% strawberry-banana juice. Now I feel like a mess. I dunno if it's the vivarin or

Cherry Bitch or the worksheets slowly making me insane. My palms are sweating silver bullets and I feel shaky and anxious. I want to write and I don't want to write. I hate this. . . . It finally wore off. Thank god. I paced around the school, then tried lying down on a couch in a teacher's room, but I couldn't calm down. My palms were sweating, then freezing, and I felt like I had a fever, and if I ever threaten to take mescaline, please stop me.

quatre.dix-huit
Camped out in front of my locker like a homeless person. Waiting for a security guard to yell at me. They pass by numerous times and do not even look at me. I should be in class. Instead, I open Bukowski's *Tales of Ordinary Madness* and read with a look of confusion on my face. I find this beautiful. No. one. notices. . . . Cherry Bitch lets me wear her cat-eyed glasses. I feel silly and vain and I like it. I walk home and eventually kiss the Wonka Boy (supposed to be gay). He shoves his tongue in my mouth anxiously, awkwardly. Too much like a child ripping open a shiny Christmas present only to be disappointed. Curry wore a candy necklace today and I tried to bite off some candy and ended up making his neck bleed. What a tragedy. My hands are cold. My feet hurt. Career week only gets worse, I think. Tomorrow we have to write notes to the presenters we saw today (like the woman from State Farm who tried to

convince us that selling insurance was a fun, interesting career field . . . LYING WHORE). That could take at least two hours. . . . vivarin. I believe this calls for vivarin.

quatre.dix-neuf

Closer to the end, but when I stick out my tongue I can't taste it. Walk home again, stopping by the wife of Burger King for an ice cream cone. Wonka Boy and Case Boy laugh. I shuffle my feet. I waste hours listening to music and packing for the beach, then braiding my hair, anxiously awaiting the last few hours of career week. Last night, at the band concert, I was confused. Vegan Grrl wraps her arms around my shoulders and holds me protectively. She smells like the earth and very cheap laundry detergent. We listen to our peers play music, resting on each other, her arm on my shoulder, my nose in her neck. It feels nice. I switch between cuddling her and sucking a boy's neck. It was a strange evening. Today lacked such oddities. It also lacked Cherry Bitch. My Greasy Buddy Holly makes nightmares and dreams more real. I question everything and eat choco-late. Thursdays are terrible days. Near the end, but not close enough to taste.

quatre.vingt-trois

The weekend finally ends. Before the memories melt together like globs of chicken fat, I would like to press my hands into the sticky wet cement for a few moments. Sleeping on the floor of Cherry Bitch's beach house right next to the giant window. Throwing my arm over her side and holding her against me. Her fingers hold my hand until they become limp one by one and I know she's fallen asleep. Wearing my brand-new Powell's sweatshirt for three days in a row. It had taffy, bodily fluids, food, sand, and dirt on it by Sunday evening. Eating ice cream cones and squeaky cheese at the Tillamook Factory.

Plum Sweater being cold and then forgiving. I nearly died. Holding Linux Shoe as I fall asleep, saddened when he's forced to go back to the boys' side of the house. Wandering up and down the beach at night in the dark listening to the waves. Bumper cars and Anti-Crombie t-shirts bought on a rainy seaside boardwalk. Cherry Bitch lighting cigarettes. Breath smelling of charcoal and ashes. Reading tarot cards for Linux Shoe and a boy who cried on the beach while holding a knife.

Monday feels like nothing in comparison. Linux Shoe dresses too nicely. I feel vague and ask for love. I am always hugging. Few arms find their way around my waist. The words become dry.

quatre.vingt-quatre
Seven weeks left of this building. I am frightened. Very frightened. Sometimes the entire world scares the crap out

of me. I still feel vague and cryptic. Season finales for all my favorite TV shows. The never-ending purr of lawn mowers in my neighborhood. Sky continually a beautiful shade of light blue. More reasons for fear. Some of my friends are driving, smoking pot, piercing their lips. I vaguely remember finger painting with tempera paints when I was seven years old. Sometimes the cycle of life makes my fingers twitch and wrists ache. A wad of dictionary pages grows larger in my stomach. I fear driving. I fear senior prom. I fear graduation. I fear college. I fear relationships. I fear life. I curl up in the fetal position on my bedroom floor, the one in the first house I lived in, the one with the elephant painted on the wall.

quatre.vingt-cinq
Enough of my philosophical rambling. Okay, that's a lie. Sometimes I'm sick of loving everyone. I'm sick of being the one people depend on. I'm sick of depending on people. I care so much the skin under my fingernails bleeds and turns black, but I am rarely held, recognized, encouraged. Sometimes loneliness makes me more vague and cryptic.

quatre.vingt-six
Linux Shoe types and sends me neatly edged words on my screen. Such words leave me in a disheveled heap of a

former person. I argue constantly with his friends (the anorexic, the Christian, the prude). They are all female and bitterly intelligent. Maybe I can't stand them because they are old-milk-flavored versions of myself and because all of them are firmly against sexuality in any form (why the hell are they friends with a fag?! Explain this to me, please.). Linux Shoe says I'm one of the last people he listens to anymore. It's sort of a compliment, but he still makes me cry. I just want to hold him until the world goes away, until there is no more pain and no people to harm him. Sometimes my fantasies are grotesque because they are never fulfilled.

quatre.vingt-sept

I type for hours and hours, putting together the literary book with clumsy fingers. My favorite part was copying dictionary pages and cutting them and pasting them back together. It is the cover of the book and I am proud. There is a punk girl with black hair. You ever notice that fat girls are never punk? It's a hard look to pull off because there's never any good funky clothing at thrift stores in large sizes. Fat people don't dress funky, just tacky. Bright neon colors and stripes. Thank God I refuse to wear clothing like that. The punk girl wears converse sneakers and mismatched socks. I admire her and wish I could dress like that. My wardrobe is too bland. I am filled with t-shirts, jeans, white underwear. I wish I could have a studded belt or a large assortment of plastic jewelry or something really defining. But I have simple pieces of average. I look in the mirror and realize, "Holy shit, I look like THEM."

cinq.sept

A few weeks later and fewer words written. guilt. Guilt. GUILT. Time has been spent contemplating, dancing around a maypole, and purchasing a 1971 light blue VW bug. Yes, ladies and gentlemen, this is my life. These things are of lesser importance and time will not be spent dwelling upon them. Instead, I would like to comment on my friends and how they fuck. No, not with cocks and cunts, but with their mouths. Their tongues flail aimlessly and they laugh and talk, but nothing is ever really said. And they never really listen either. I frustrate myself to no end trying to talk to them and help them through the problems they create and refuse to solve. This is called being a teenager, I'm told, though I don't quite understand it. They never listen. Their tongues keep pressing against their teeth and lips and they keep fucking with their mouths like there is no tomorrow, but they don't know how to communicate. Just fuck. Watching them at lunchtime is like a really messy kinky porn. I can see dicks being jammed in cunts, lifeless bodies smacking into each other, using one another, and nothing being accomplished. Not one thing being done. Not one idea being communicated. But there is a lot of useless rubbing, grinding, laughing, and spilling of unnecessary liquids. I turn my head to my Linux Shoe and cry, but my tears never hit the formica table.

cinq.huit

My Linux Shoe is melancholy and I do not know how to help it. I get annoyed, push him away, give up. I tell him he is margarine, that he is my only joy and other contradictory things. High school poetry slam in thirteen days and I'm sure it will mostly be trembling teenagers reciting poorly written love poems in crackly voices. I think it will be marvelous. I'm going to read one of Linux Shoe's poems and a few other writings. . . . I have this feeling that I am running around and accomplishing nothing. This is springtime. I must resist the urge to place daisies in gun barrels. Last night my dad was driving me home from band practice and we passed by a fast-food joint. EIGHT FUCKING COP CARS WERE THERE TO BUST TWO GUYS! TWO! I counted. Pigs. Goddamn pigs. I felt like screaming but I couldn't. My dad is the only one who would say, "Hey, wanna go back and look at what happened?" My mother would never do such a thing. She usually comes home, lights a cigarette, drinks liquor diluted in cheap soda, and reads crime novels. She is not a bad person. I worry that she is too unhappy. Case Boy has decided to make a political statement by wearing the same outfit every day until school ends. I admire his philosophy, though fear it is misguided. A girl named Louisa wore the same green dress every day in the fall. These girls in my biology class were talking about her. "Isn't that strange? I want to ask her about it, blah blah blah." (More mouth fucking, you know.) I calmly interrupted, "Why does it matter? Why do you care?" And the girl with flat brown hair and boring lips sneers, "Oh, I don't care, I just want to know why she'd do that. It's weird." These people drive me crazy.

cinq.neuf

One day closer to Wonka Boy's birthday. I regret this fact and try to avoid it. I asked my mother if she would ground me and she refused. I should go, she says, to support him. Support his masochism? His ignorance? His naiveté? I don't have patience for him. Or Case Boy. Or for Curry. Linux Shoe is the only one I enjoy sometimes, and even then my patience runs thin. He explains that he is not pretty enough, even though he is so gorgeous it hurts my eyes. He does not understand this. He does not believe me. I cannot explain the pain this causes. I scratch at that soft spot in the middle of my palm, the place that I scratch but it does not really itch, and I try to think of ways to get out of his party. I'll probably end up going. I'll probably end up slipping paxil into his drink just to keep him calm. "Are you guys having fun?" "What do you want to do?" Every five minutes. Just give him more paxil. Things will be FINE. Right. Tomorrow is "field day," a random day of chaos where I'm sure the security guards will be prodding us from one place to another. I think I'll use the time to do my homework, instead of watching teachers get dunked or the car show or the pudding contest or any of the other things that make me sunburned. That's tomorrow and I should not bother worrying about it today. Highlight of today: Case Boy giving a three-minute speech in about two breaths and one sentence (imagine a drunk chipmunk on a bottle of caffeine pills).

cinq.onze
I worry about very, very tedious things. My friends are very, very horny. And sometimes, if I listen closely enough, I can't hear anything at all. I can hear black. Linux Shoe nods and tells me I think too much and say too little. I never thought of myself as such a person but he is right. Sometimes I don't say what I think. That makes me human. He comes over and we sit in my 1970-something bug and listen to the radio. The seats aren't even cracked. We ride public transportation and eat Mexican food and look at books and boys. He is not perfect. But he's the closest thing I've found.

cinq.quatorze

I manage to fuck up everything. It's a talent of mine, I'm incredibly proud of it. Forget writing. I'm going to be a professional incarnation of Loki, destroying everything I can. My mother makes another trite suggestion, hates her job, the way her husband comes home too late, and five hundred other things. I roll my eyes, say fuck once or twice, and mortally wound her. Something about her cookies and how I do not want meat and other crap and will she please just give me the money so I can do it myself. She turns to me, glass coffeepot in hand, telling me to leave before she throws something at me. I can hear her blubbering to my father over the phone. I sigh. I fuck up everything. It's a talent of mine.

cinq.dix-huit

My counselor is covering tables with paper for senior awards night. She asks for help. I tell her I will have no part in it. She says that someday I may be at the awards night. I tell her that when I'm there, I won't sit at a table covered with fucking paper. How many yards of that shit did she waste? I don't want to know. She doesn't know what I was talking about, just like my biology teacher. We were discussing natural selection and evolution. She said people become immune to bacteria thanks to antibiotics and we keep evolving. She also said that people took a lot of unnecessary drugs, which only pushed evolution even farther. I made a comment about prescription drugs being advertised, more immunities created, side effects quickly mumbled, and the eventual deterioration of the human body. She looks at me like I'm crazy and tells me that I'm not talking about anything relevant. I think she's still upset 'cause I read magazines while she's giving lectures and still receive high scores on the quizzes. Well, I would get higher scores if the fucking bitch didn't count taking notes as part of the grade. (A nostalgic friend tells me that when he was my age, girls didn't write about tongues, rotten vegetables, and other inappropriate subjects.)

cinq.vingt-et-un

I do not spend time in class today. . . . I spend time in the lecture room, arranging black lights, feathers hanging from the ceiling, scribbling art with chalk. The room is art nouveau. Wonderful, as Cherry Bitch would say. Later that evening, she dons a pair of wings and white clothing which electrifies under the black light (scotch tape does too). It is a slam. A slamming sort of slam. I read first, pieces I pretend are my own. Lips I pretend are my own. A voice I pretend is my own. The band drifts between my words (the beat of a drum and the hum of a strum of a guitar . . .). Absolutely fabulous, as Cherry Bitch would say. Later, I win a prize for best reading voice. Curry wins a prize for best overall piece.

Flecks of spit hit the microphone as he recites his acceptance speech: "Holy crap." I laugh. Linux Shoe wears a wine-colored shirt (I swoon) and the evening is absolutely wonderful. The room is humid and quite moist, but the atmosphere is perfect. . . . I'd die in that room, if I had a choice.

cinq.vingt-trois
Every day at lunch, Jar Guard eats two pieces of fruit, fat-free yogurt, or some other tasteless dish. He screws up his face in disgust. I tell him that I would never put him on a diet. I want to marry a man like him. Soft but not fat. Intelligent but not arrogant. Owns a sticker that says "Tough Guys Write Poetry." Black hair and funky glasses. Wears pin-striped pants, shiny black shoes, and casual-dress shirts. He's only been teaching for three years, so he isn't burned out yet. One of the few teachers who still seems alive. If I were a teacher, I would lose all hope very quickly. I lost all hope as a student quite a while ago. He continues to smile and walks with his shoulders back, hips moving. And maybe because he remembers those random things that mean everything. "You're a very beautiful woman," he tells me. I smile too, for the first time in months.

cinq.vingt-quatre
Techno Boy, the one who took me to McDonald's so long ago, gives me a ride home in his air-conditioned car.

Reluctantly, I agree to go home with him. He does not want to be alone but he does not say so. His parents collect porcelain figures with rosy cheeks. Cats, women, bears, pigs. All made of pale ceramic. He claims they are worth upward of three hundred dollars. I've never trusted people who so greatly value material possessions. Value them enough to choke their homes with them. He shows me the basement: twenty thousand heaving worn brown boxes filled to the brim with Christmas decorations, more porcelain figurines arranged on shelves, and two separate bullet-making contraptions. I feel overwhelmed. I think his house would make a wonderful bonfire. I simply nod. His hands shake very, very badly all the time. He tried to move out of his parents' house because they are verbally abusive. He tried to smile when he showed me his bedroom, Shari's menu laying on the floor (I have to memorize it for work, he tells me. I open it up and ask, How much is a Denver omelette? He smiles painfully, "six forty-nine?" I tell him he is right, even though he is fifty cents off.).

cinq.vingt-cinq

I do not spend time in class today because there are no classes. I wake up late, make omelettes with Linux Shoe, then go downtown with Wonka Boy and Case Boy. We go everywhere, as far as we can go by public transportation.

We eat Mexican food, buy rainbows and buttons that define us. (Linux Shoe is a pink triangle.) I wear jean shorts and birkenstocks. I wonder if I am . . . defined. I ask random questions as we wander. . . . "Have you ever loved anyone?" . . . "What do you fear the most?" . . . I discover they have never loved anyone and they fear nothing (everything). That evening Curry comes over and we all watch movies. My mother finds it difficult to have him in the house, but she tries. He is calm and we seem shocked. We have to do things, or things will never change. So I rest my head on his leg and he pets my hair. We suck food off each other's fingers at the suggestion of Linux Shoe. I still feel like I'm jumping on an elevator—weightless and pulled down at the same time.

cinq.vingt-six

Linux Shoe points out that for Curry, they've won. Curry writes poetry about girls with bubblegum brains and fleeting democracy and uses *fuck* like he invented it. These things are in his mind. He hates them, he obsesses about them, he writes teenagerish poetry about them. They've won. The politicians, the stupid girls, the angry boys, they've all won. He is so right. All I can do is nod. Curry has given up and let them win and Linux Shoe knows this and he says so. It's so much easier and so much more difficult to let them go. They're going to grow up and live and die and consume. So why rage at them? They are frustrating and annoying. But writing lame poetry and toiling solves nothing. So let it go. He wears his Old Navy and drinks his twenty-four-ounce lattes from Starbucks while hatefully condemning all of society. Why? Because THEY are so trite and ignorant. Like listening to Bad Religion makes him some sort of pseudo anarchist god. Okay, so maybe I exaggerate a little. He isn't that bad. But some people are. A stoner girl in a few of my classes hates the popular people who wear converse shoes. Like when you go to buy converse shoes, she thinks you should have to show your anarchy-punk ID card. Another girl in our class wears converse shoes and gap jeans, an ultimate sin to the punk stoner girl. All I wanna know, all I really wanna know is: When the fuck is this shit going to matter? Jesus Christ, people, let it go. Let it be.

cinq.vingt-neuf

I yell at Wonka Boy today. Case Boy points out that I haven't given up because I still care. I turn my head away and scowl because he is right. I am either too cold and shut off and hateful, or I am too loving and I care too much and I am too empathetic. I do not have peace. I do not have a medium. I tell Wonka Boy he wears my patience thin. He smirks, bites at my tongue with a lisp, tries so hard to be sassy. I want to slap him. I want to wake him up. I realize I am still trying. Like Linux Shoe tells me, I want to fix every-thing for everyone. I give them logical solutions and I don't understand when they can't follow through. Linux Shoe tells me that they know how to solve their problems and they choose not to. I have to believe him. I have to believe him or my tongue will bleed like bright red kool-aid.

cinq.trente

I watch a movie called *Edge of Seventeen*. I feel like I'm going to be sick and that's okay. Instead of eating too much, I'm thinking too much and I need to throw up some of these thoughts before something vile happens. I am think-ing that I don't need to prove myself to the people who don't matter. I am thinking that I love Linux Shoe and he could be taken away from me at any moment. I am think-ing of longing. I am thinking that I would like to be six years old or nineteen years old. I am thinking I am indeci-sive. Mostly I am longing. I am convincing myself of many, many things, but my longing is a constant. My longing is riding my bike with pink streamers on the handles to 7-11 and buying a slurpee. My longing is a soft boy to hold me. My longing is to be rid of my empathy. Out of all the things I am thinking and convincing myself of, the only thing I know for sure is that it's okay. It's okay to convince and to long and to think. And perhaps most important, I know what matters. Linux Shoe matters. My words matter. The people I love matter. Not that building, not those letters on that piece of paper, not the teachers who yell, not the teachers who tape pictures of pretty blond girls to their podiums, not the crackly voice on the PA, not the scores from the "state," not the stupid girls or the angry boys. As simple as this may be, I sit and cry because no one else will know this for a very, very long time. . . . I know a billion other truths and philosophical ramblings. But what do I really know? Nothing. I'm fourteen. I am a girl in a pretty little public high school in a pretty little house in a pretty little neighborhood. What do I know?

cinq.trente-et-un

Outside the window a group of seniors are making a video, presumably for some sort of class project. I know most of their names, which surprises even me. Sometimes I feel like a child sitting on the ground, fingers reaching upward, grasping at the sky, but it's always just a little bit out of reach. My mother tells me I am too young to know what is dangerous. I disagree. I can see danger when I turn my head. I see danger in the fifteen-year-old girls with perfectly rounded breasts who wear strapless tops and shorts on ninety-degree days. I see them getting raped in the back of a car without air conditioning. I see danger in the boys who drive the black pickup truck with twenty-five friends in the back and an easily abused PA system. I see danger in the teacher who ignores the vibrating tension of his own class-room. My civics teacher astounds me because, at times, he is anything but civil. Earlier this year, two girls were snapping at each other from across the room. "Don't talk shit about me! I'm gonna beat you up, bitch!" Snotty giggling ensued from the other side of the room. The teacher rolled his eyes and continued lecturing, only once pausing to ask them to "quiet down." As soon as the girls left the room, they started fighting. Jar Guard had to pull the whitetrashboxergirl off the richblondgirl. Thank God for American noneducation.

six.un

He wears black clothing. He is socialistically inclined. He smokes cigarettes (when he puts the right end in his mouth). He drinks iced coffee. He was born in 1974. (Let's call him Raskolnikov.) But this does not matter to me. I shuffle through the rain in my birkenstocks and enjoy the warm squish beneath my feet. I purposely walk in the rain and not under the awning. I walk in the rain. I walk in the rain, tilt my head up to the sky, and taste someone's tears.

six.deux

I arrive at the movie theater almost completely drenched. You know how you watch the news and you hear about hikers who get lost? And you always think, "Gosh, they're dumb." Yeah. Well. Not as hard as it seems. It pours hail and rain. We laugh and run through open fields and listen to the thunder. The earth club does have its high points, when we're not digging through garbage cans. *Shrek*. Drek. Crap. I go to a movie with wet hair and Curry lets me kiss his neck. I push him away. When I come home, I bring my fingers to my nose and smell his cologne. I can't stop smelling his cologne.

six.trois

Linux Shoe and I go to the temple (spell it. pee oh double-you eee ell ell sss). We look at boys. They look at us. We ride the MAX. We look at them. They look at us. There is a particularly attractive young man in a suit. We look at him. He looks out the window. I could go on for days describing people on the MAX. I am particularly curious about the people who take out cigarettes and twirl them between their fingers nervously. They stand as close to the door as they can get, faces nearly smashed up against the glass. Even before the door opens, they light their cigarettes and take a few drags. I've seen this more than once. It makes me think of Raskolnikov and the cat hair on his pants. It makes me think of the girl with stringy blond hair and glasses. It makes me think of the blue-haired girl with a lip ring eating brownies. It makes me think of the sexy Russian talking on his cell phone in his Adidas jacket. It makes me think of the old Asian ladies whose feet didn't touch the floor. It makes me think of a freckled girl and her fag, holding hands and looking away from each other.

six.cinq

I read the things I wrote a month ago. A year ago. Five seconds ago. I eat oatmeal in the morning and wonder how many mornings I'll eat oatmeal. I wonder how many mornings it will be until I am serving oatmeal to my kids. Three minutes ago I was in kindergarten, following plastic footprints of the imaginary classroom leprechaun. I have sixty seconds until I graduate. When I microwave water and press the faded white buttons for a minute-forty-five, I realize that two minutes are slipping away. Then nine minutes. And then I get my degree and marry some boy and I am scooping up sand off the beach with my fingers wide open and everything is slipping through. You can't hold on to anything for longer than it is happening. Nineteen minutes from now, I'm going to die. And in the next millisecond, nothing will matter. Not a thing.

six.six

Teachers are asking for reflective writing now. Something nice to make them look good. Hah. Midwestern Tackiness asks for our dreams, hopes, and goals and tells us to look back at what we wrote in September. I look at what I wrote when I was little, nine months ago. From what I've written,

I sound exactly the same. But 5,418 different things have happened since then. I wonder if I am constant. I wonder if this is a bad thing. I still like alternative rock. I still dislike ignorant and closed-minded people. I still like reading. I am so bland, whitewash milk water of a girl. I am not the September girl. I am the June girl. And tomorrow I will be the July girl. And three days after that I'll be gone. I don't like writing about my goals and reflective writing and other such things. When I was in the sixth grade we had to set goals for ourselves and I didn't know what to write. I showed up to class every day, I learned everything I could, I got near-perfect scores on everything. To me, I didn't know how to improve. And my teachers let me think that, too. If I could, I would touch that girl's cheek very gently and ask her some very difficult questions. But she left me a long time ago. I'm the June girl now. I've got leftist magazines and strange poetry and birkenstocks. I'm that June girl.

six.sept
I only get halfway through the day before I leave. Well, everyone else leaves too. I don't understand why we have TWO half days of school in a row. Why not just one day without school instead of two incredibly short days which everyone skips? (Except for me, I've got guilt that tastes like safety pins.) I go downtown and my mother warns me about the fleet coming in for Rose Festival. "Watch out for

the sailors." Yes, Mother, I want to say, I'll take some rub-bers with me. Sometimes I think I'm just a tad too sour. I go to my temple alone and find older boys there. The first one is Raskolnikov and this does not surprise me because I am looking for him. I find him dressed in his traditional black attire poking at a bookshelf in a room the color of the ocean. I walk quietly, wondering how close I can get to him before he notices. We sit at a table near the window and the sun bakes me gently like a rotisserie chicken. He drinks iced coffee and lets me look at his wallet. He picks up his cup and moves it slightly to the left with his left hand, then taps the table with his right hand, fingers squished together, clipped fingernails tapping on the glass surface. I lose count of how many times he does this. Greasy Buddy Holly appears from nowhere with his lisp and tortoiseshell glasses. I pin him up against a wall, shine a light in his face, and ask him everything. Some days it's really nice to forget who I am. Some days it's really nice to pretend that I've got another life without obligations—a life with books and men in their twenties and thirties and music and talking and words. But then I have to leave to go to band rehearsal. it. all. comes. crashing.

six.huit
I don't understand why my civics teacher even gives a final. He asks students if they would like to take it. I had the option to not take the test but I did anyway. WHY AM I SO

LAME? Perhaps a better question: WHY IS MY TEACHER SO LAME? I answer all the questions, even the essay ones (but I do so spitefully, inserting bits of liberalistic rambling). It's the end of the year now, only a few more days to go. No one cares about the dress code (not that they ever did). My eyes burn with images of strapless tops and young breasts and tanned legs and thighs and sandals and painted toenails. I imagine that the male teachers must walk around with near-constant erections. I have no pity for them.

six.neuf

Stepping in horseshit is never as glamorous as it seems. Stepping in horseshit when you're behind a float that leaks water is even less glamorous, if you can imagine. I have no appetite when it is over. I just want to go home and sit. I want to pretend that I am not such a band geek and that I do not spend my Saturdays wearing a shako and playing a brass instrument. But sometimes life is like that. I don't get much choice. I come home, try to clean myself of the stench (band geek or horseshit—I can't tell which is worse, so I scrub extra hard). I have to leave soon, anyway, to go burn dead animal flesh with the literary department from school. We listen to Bob Dylan and talk about what is important and play basketball and I touch my Linux Shoe until my hands bleed rose petals. He is leaving for Singapore on Wednesday. He matters to me like my shoelaces. Always there, always wrapped between the holes. Everything falls apart when he's gone. I can't walk. I trip and fall and lick the ground. After the BBQ, I continue to be a teenager. We go to a double feature at a cheesy theater in the ghetto part of the suburbs. I remember being little and thinking that the teenagers who sat in the back row were obnoxious and stupid and I never wanted to be like them. I am, now. We laugh and rest our feet on the backs of the seats. We throw candy and poke each other. I wonder how long I can do this before I am the adult sitting in front of myself, rolling my eyes and just wanting to watch the movie. The second movie is so bad we leave during the middle and wander around the empty streets. I'm not too scared because one boy has a knife. We act like teenagers. We do stupid things. One girl steals a letter off a sign and puts it in her purse. We go into a food mart at a gas station and laugh at the condoms for sale. We walk by a pizza joint and I wave like a freak at a friend inside. I run in and talk with her, thinking that I never would have done this a year ago when I hated these sort of people. When I called them stupid and immature. When I hated them so much for having fun. I've only got three years, one month, and sixteen days left of this. I'm not going to waste it anymore.

six.douze—the last day
I am writing these words with a swollen tongue. It's very difficult to put all this into sentences. I'm swimming in my

45

thoughts and struggling to pick just one. I'll start somewhere.

After finishing my last final of my freshman year, I am not contemplative. I am a bit dazed. Linux Shoe hands me his shiny black jacket and I breathe it in. He leaves tomorrow. I come home and sit in the silence. I listen as hard as I can. I read the senior edition of the school newspaper. All the seniors were asked about their most embarrassing moments, best memories, and future plans. I smile at their "future plans." They're all so little. Some want to "sleep" and "get fat" and "get married" and quite a few said, "I have no idea." I wonder about my future plans in four years. I wonder about my best memories and embarrassing moments and pep rallies and football games. I smile because for some people this is everything. Everything. And their life is ending because this is everything. When they fall to their knees and sob, I touch the tops of their heads and keep walking.

I go to graduation tonight. It's even more depressing than last year. Vegan Grrl gives a lengthy speech about the Dalai Lama, Zen, world peace, climbing trees, and catastrophic atrocities. Most of the audience stares blankly, including her peers in the front row. I applaud when she finishes. I applaud when she wins an award. I applaud when she gets a diploma. My hands are raw and sore after all of this. My eyes are too. How many more graduations can I watch before I'm walking across the stage? I look at my hands again. I wonder if they are my own. Later, I come home and laugh at my principal for denying a girl her diploma. I laugh at his raspy southern accent. I laugh because he mimics Bush Jr. unconsciously. It's sort of embarrassing when my political and educational leaders cannot verbalize their thoughts without drooling. But I digress.

They yell and hug and celebrate the fact that they're grown up and they've done so much and it's all been so hard and I watch very, very quietly. If I'm quiet enough, maybe I can slip away and I won't have to do it too. Like when you were in kindergarten and you didn't want to share so you just said, "Pass." When they call my name to get my diploma, I'll say, "Pass." When they call my name to make me grow up, I'll say, "Pass." No one made you do it if you said pass.

I'd like to sum it all up in a really prophetic way, but I can't. I'm fourteen. I don't know anything. The truly beautiful thing is that I can admit it. And I've got a long, long time to learn everything. I've got my lips and my pen and my birkenstocks and my Linux Shoe and my books and my temple made of pages and words and shelves. These things matter to me now. Maybe they won't in ten years or yesterday or in the next half hour. But right now, this very second, I know what matters.

Linux Shoe once told me my hands and lips are roses. My hands and lips are blooming.

"A word of caution is in order at this point."
—Stephen R. Matt, *Electricity and Basic Electronics*

NEW CHARACTERS

scully/skull—first girlfriend turned first boifriend. robot fetishist, girl punk rocker, dance revolution addict. kissed the mix CDs she made for me and stole my heart. kissed my lips and stole my brain. became a boy and turned me straight.

go—enemy turned friend. brave enough to hold my hand. too scared to admit what she wants and hates. frantic, dramatic hummingbird on crack with a megaphone. perfect handwriting and genius scrambled eggs for brains.

eve—girl with a car and a paycheck. purchases empathic ice cream from the same diner every week. sings with her heart and throat, loves with her lips and mind. I am afraid to kiss her.

maple bar—girlfriend of Eve. rainbow hair and metal through her ears and eyebrow. jingles when she walks, metal clinking against metal. went to college to learn puns.

tupperware—Buddhist best friend. twentysomething writer with a lotus-blossom heart. my tranquilizer, confidant, and comedian. olive juice.

grandpa—history teacher with 'Nam flashbacks and a hatred of capitalism. rants daily about Bush, Enron, Al Qaeda, and mass consumption of everything by Americans.

paul revere—a costume worn by a boy. opens his mouth only to warn others that the British are coming and we pray together that it isn't too late.

british boy—one night with his hands down Paul Revere's pajamas and he loses everything. rapist. vile and disgusting.

old man—rims poke through the tire tread of his heart. about to have a blow out. how many more miles can he go? tired and aching and trying, trying, trying. saving sinking-ship students. one-man lifeboat.

margot—tiny feet in thrift-store cowboy boots and barely there chest covered by small cotton t-shirts. has perfect lips and frightens boys. knows every line to *The Royal Tenenbaums*.

poke—a boy with a beard and a guitar.

CELEBRITY CAMEOS

thea hillman—lesbian goddess, intersex activist, lovely lady, true Trope fan.

justin chin—poet with elves who live in his ass. mystical, talented, and gay, much like Tom Cruise, but not.

6.15
cracked coffee-cream lips,

Poetry won't come from my lips or hands. All the words have been for my small press book, which might be born in September. I don't know if I've got enough words left for poetry. I could press the quill against my tongue and try to make it bleed ink, but I just scratch my tongue and taste copper.

Ice cubes are melting in a large clear glass to my left. I'm using it to numb my tongue so I can stab it with that quill again. I'll be able to write again, just wait. Just wait.

very thin burrito wrapper,

caryatid

6.17
cracked coffee-cream lips,

My burned flesh is bright pink, dotted meticulously

with brown blotches. I think my lips got burned too. I like to sit in the dark now, looking at the sun, not being a part of it.

My knees and heels are quite raw from walking on pavement stuck together like rice krispies squares. Spongy when you bounce. My cheeks hurt from smiling.

Important fact learned today: There is a state ordinance that says that topless women must have their nipples covered.

half-full bottle of perfume,
caryatid

6.18
cracked coffee-cream lips,

Tomboy lesbians in white Adidas shoes with sharp spiky hair and sometimes glasses break my heart. Maybe I'm just a stupid lipstick lesbian. Or bisexual. Or something.

If I was a gay man, I could be catty and witty and bitchy and gay and it could be so much fun. I'd actually have a reason to be at a pride parade instead of just being . . . confused. Or a supporter. Or an onlooker. I could be there 'cause, dammit, I would be a gay man! And I'd dress so well. I'd have a dick that would be to die for and swanky hips and, fuck it, guys would want me!

So what's the solution? I'll just, uh, stick with the word *bisexual* and say it very very quietly and be the best fag hag this world has ever seen. Margaret Cho, watch out.

I miss you, faggot. My faggot. My dear sweet perfect fag. Come home soon and tell me about the cocks you'd like to suck.

lips sticky with iced tea,

caryatid

P.S. I'm in love with this girl. You would adore her. Absolutely adore her.

6.19

cracked coffee-cream lips,

A butch girl in khaki shorts and a yellow polo shirt asked me for a string of my Mardi Gras beads.

"If I give them to you, what do I get?" My only attempt at being flirtatious all day.

"What do you want?" Her thick lips stretched into a grin.

I want you to fall in love with me and I want you to know everything about me and I want you to put your tongue in my mouth, my heart, my brain. I want you. I want you.

I handed her the beads with a cowardly smile and she walked away.

Come with me next year and make me brave.

thinking about the "kisses for pride" table,

caryatid

✦✦

cracked coffee-cream lips,

I had a dream. A real dreaming sort of dream. Before you were there I can remember small bits and pieces. Kissing a boy with a very angular mouth. Kissing another boy with a softer mouth. This is very frustrating and it makes my palms itch. When you arrive in my dream, I cling to you. You tell me that you were driven here from Singapore, that it's only an hour away but you can't stay long. We lie on my bed and I hold you so tight.

My eyes keep welling up with tears but I can't quite cry. A swollen lump just beneath my throat is waiting to explode. And, oh, lord, does it hurt. How many more weeks without you? Oh, Linux Shoe, baby. Why'd you do this? It feels good to be in love with the world but you aren't home and that makes it difficult. I'm in love with you the most. And it's not something that I had to try to do or work at or even something that grew or expanded, it just simply was. I said, "Hello, here's my heart, you can have it. You're the only one who deserves it."

My hands and lips are wilting without you. Slowly curling into themselves and becoming rustic-looking. My perfect adorable homosexual . . . The words are dry without you.

losing this game,
caryatid

6.20

cracked coffee-cream lips,

Eve offered to buy me ice cream and let me look at her underwear. She's my brother's friend but she's cute and bisexual and I balled up a straw wrapper and dropped it down the front of her dress, right between her breasts. My brother's face exploded with blood and embarrassment. Teeth crunching on the ice in my water glass, she tells me: "Chewing on ice is a way to relieve sexual tension." In her blue dress and plastic sandals, she tells me: "I think you're cool."

following you,
caryatid

✦✦

cracked coffee-cream lips,

A boy got on the train today with a small wooden drum. Noise was wrapped around his head and a musical note on his ankle. This boy tattooed music on his body, carried it with him, put it in his head. But his drum, Linux, baby, was broken. His drum was broken. The leather stretched over the drum was torn. He could wear and hear music but he couldn't make it. I wanted to cry.

wanting to throw up falafel,
caryatid

6.22

cracked coffee-cream lips,

There's this boy at the library who looks like Harry Potter. He's got big glasses and pointy elbows and messy brown hair. I watched him while he shelved books. I watched him bend over and push the books into their place. It made me want him.

Music today is Gus Gus and words are from Bukowski. He tells me that what matters most is how well I walk through the fire but I'm burning and turning crisp like bacon.

8:45 A.M. on Tuesday morning, my mother will put me on a plane and ship me off like cargo to a family I've never met. Friends of hers from high school, she promises I'll get along with their daughters.

Cherry loves the manuscript. Of course. She calls me her Bukowski. She promises to give me a kiss before I die.

I'm waiting for a lot of things. Just. waiting.

her hand was on crushed black velvet,

caryatid

6.25

cracked coffee-cream lips,

Swimming in the middle of open CD cases, clothes on the floor, hair ties, books, papers, and even more nameless objects. What should stay and what should go? I wish I could decide.

The plane takes off tomorrow but it probably won't be able to get off the ground with everything I want to take with me.

Pens, paper, envelopes, addresses. I'm going to write as much as possible with my fat blank notebook and inky pens and $110. I can pay someone to write for me.

I chewed the skin off around one of my fingernails today. I don't know why. I just kept chewing at it, even though it hurt.

I'll be back July tenth with a notebook full of writing and skin the color of tomatoes.

biting the canker sore on her lower lip,

caryatid

6.26

cracked coffee-cream lips,

I've got to tell you about these boys in the airport, on the airplane, inside my phone. I'm sitting by the emergency exit, taking off backward. I'm thinking about you in Singapore. They're talking about the flight to Sacramento (I'm going to Ontario) and things to do in case the world explodes. The flotation device under your seat, baby, it's all about that flotation device. "In case of Apocalypse, please exit through one of the six bulletproof glass windows." Indeed. Like it would do any good. So, these boys. He was with his mom and sister. Icon of troubled teenagerdom.

Dressed very simply in a black sweatshirt, black jeans, black shoes, black backpack. He waited in line with his mom and sister (both appropriately attired in conservative gap uniforms), got coffee and pastries from Coffee People (I got a large hot chocolate with whipped cream). I watched as they went to Wendy's so he could get a hamburger and a coke. Too beautiful. Just too good. I've had, maybe, three-four hours of sleep but I feel perfect. There are people here I need to write about but I'm not sure how. She's got bright red-grape-colored hair spiked up like Poke's. Sigh. And another boy is covered with tattoos and large wooden loops stretching his earlobes open. I tell my mother I'm going to sit next to him and make him my boyfriend. Oh, and my brother knows about my crush on Plum Sweater.

wishing for a wallet photograph,
caryatid

✦✦

cracked coffee-cream lips,

So I lived and the plane didn't crash. The girls, Fifteen and Thirteen, are more and less what I expected. Fifteen smokes, drinks, goes to boys' houses, doesn't like school. Thirteen is bubbly and cute. They are close. Fifteen thinks I'm boring. I don't smoke pot or cigarettes or drink so what am I supposed to do around here? I'm too much for them.

Pardon me for being unamused by her bored-girl-in-hot-little-town-smoking-Marlboros attitude.

living,

caryatid

6.27

cracked coffee-cream lips,

Currently wearing a white t-shirt, green khakis, birks, dirty feet. Listening to Harvey Danger. Wanting things I can't have. Like you. Like the familiarity of home and my phone and being close enough to lie sufficiently to my parents. To give you a small idea, the girls are the annoyed Californian type—preppy kind of punk rawk that everyone hates. They listen to bad music and drink and smoke really cheap cigarettes. The smell burns on my lips. I wish I could get along with them. I'm just the "quiet" cousin. I have nothing to say around them. Nothing. After dinner I'm going to call my mother and tell her I have too much to complain about after two days. You keep getting farther away. Farther and farther.

pow!

caryatid

6.30

cracked coffee-cream lips,

In my dreams, Joaquin Phoenix kisses me but when I wake up he isn't there and you aren't either and I'm inside a sweaty tent on an inflatable mattress with everything sticking to my skin. Bugs are crawling on me.

A tent, not puplike,

caryatid

7.1

cracked coffee-cream lips,

I sunburned my mouth. Made some art. Fucked up everyone. Just another day. I'm going to bed now before this letter turns to shit like everything else I've touched.

caryatid

7.7

cracked coffee-cream lips,

I'm a failure. I couldn't take Fifteen and Thirteen and their dysfunctional family any longer so I left to visit my grandparents and left them to visit more relatives. Fifteen/Thirteen's father seemed hurt and I didn't care. It's gone and I'll never have to see them again or yawn as she lights up another Marlboro, her sister watching with round eyes.

waiting for the day *fag* is a verb,

caryatid

P.S. I think it's required that the boys who work at Trader Joe's must 1) be absolutely adorable in some strange way and 2) smell like granola.

Cherry,

I was in Trader Joe's today. I bought cherry popsicles because of you. JUST because of you. I buy cherryheads when I see them, even though they aren't as good as lemonheads. Cherry suckers. Cherry candy of any sort. There was a commercial for Bing cherries ($3.49 a pound) on TV.

Maybe, if I pretend enough, and taste you in my mouth enough, you'll come home sooner.

I miss you, Cherry girl.

tasting so many imitations,

caryatid

P.S. I know you're beautiful in Europe. I want pictures above my fireplace. I want giant life-size portraits. I want cardboard cutouts.

7.10

cracked coffee-cream lips,

In air-conditioning with boxes of words all around me. The man at the desk gives me old looks. Very old looks. Hands still shaking and I think I have a sunburn. Can't stand sitting here because I can't move to see things better. To see people better. Quite frustrating. Oh, wow he's cute. Glasses, brown hair, spiked blond bangs, and a chain clinging to his black jean shorts. He sat at a computer and now I can't see.

$^2/_3$ actual size,

caryatid

✦✦

cracked coffee-cream lips,

Bukowski had a lot of women. I wonder if I were alive back then and I showed up at his door and offered myself to him if he'd have me. How many cherries has Bukowski popped, I wonder. What about mine?

part john,

caryatid

7.11

cracked coffee-cream lips,

I'm very much in love. Someone this morning asked me with what, with whom. Why one thing? Why one person?

I think if people read that I'm "in love" they'll think I'm taken. Why do people assume that love is a subtractive thing? If I'm in love with one thing or person, I don't have enough love for something else? Bullshit. Utter bullshit. Every time I fall in love with something, someone, I have that much more love all over again.

Teenagers shouldn't write about love, ever. They sound

like pineapples in a blender on Christmas morning.

friends don't let friends write about love campaign 2001,

caryatid

7.12

cracked coffee-cream lips,

Cherry is home. We miss you. She got her hair cut really short apparently, and they did other ugly things to her. Wanna know what's weird? I bet she's too damn gorgeous, no matter what. She could shave her head and walk around naked and I'd fall at her feet.

if I touch you, you'll smile,

caryatid

7.14

His voice is away in Singapore with his words and his lips. His hands, the ones with the dry palms, the ones that play the cello, the ones that play with the curls in my hair, are in Singapore. And I've got this big hole in the stomach, growing larger, aching every day. When I told my friends that he said my hands and lips were roses, they all "oohed" and said how wonderful he must be, how lucky I am, how they must meet him to determine his intentions. His intentions, I hope, include Mexican food, books, my bug, and San Francisco. Ow. Goddamn ulcer. You, Linux, are my fucking ulcer.

7.15

cracked coffee-cream lips,

Plum Sweater and I tried to find the Spaghetti Factory but she's directionally challenged and I don't drive and then Greasy Buddy Holly called and we gave up and went to Maya's instead. Taco salad and black beans, she talks about a school that she won't be a part of anymore. We went to the Sexual Minority Youth Recreation Center afterward and I had the pleasure of hearing her say she's "questioning," but when the evening was over I still didn't have the courage to kiss her on the cheek.

you're always leaving and I'm always waiting,
caryatid

7.16

cracked coffee-cream lips,

Poke is lovely. We went to Borders, where they told me that I am not old enough to buy an R-rated movie. My father told me that if anyone ever asks how old I am, I should reply, "How old do I look?" My smart mouth was not smart enough and my cheeks burned red.

Poke casually mentions that he would like to put his weiner in my butt while eating chocolate and sipping a root beer. I smirk and think of his girlfriend, whose parents are Sufis and are relocating to Napa Valley in August. He says he's going to miss her and I don't think he could ever love me.

It rained.

Hey, fucker, I miss you.

boycott Borders,

caryatid

7.17

cracked coffee-cream lips,

Woke up feeling like someone had beaten me with a sack of potatoes. Soft and sore everywhere. Today I will: go to the library, write, live, come home, read, and try to fix my manuscript. Tomorrow I will: get my fucking manuscript to Greasy Buddy Holly or else.

My head is a big gray cloud right now. Do you think it will rain?

singing love songs,

caryatid

7.18

cracked coffee-cream lips,

This manuscript is never going to reach his hands.

Wonka Boy and Case Boy will never reconcile.

My book will never be published.

No one will ever love me.

Greasy Buddy Holly will never like the art.

We will never agree on a title.

I will never find a boy.

I will never be skinny.

Curry will never give me up.

Case Boy will never have his heart broken.

My brother will never find a girlfriend.

We will never eat at Maya's again.

We will never go boy hunting again.

You will never wear your pin again.

You are never coming home.

You are never coming home.

caryatid

7.19

cracked coffee-cream lips,

I keep thinking about when you get home and how happy I'll be. Except that it will be August 7. And the summer will nearly be over. And I'll be starting band camp soon after. And then my sophomore year. And it. will. snowball. Until I'm twenty-five and burned out and wishing I were fourteen again.

I turn fifteen in six days. Oh, God. This girl, at the library, was seven years old. I'm TWICE her age. Oh, shit. What were you doing when you were seven? I was finger painting.

the tank is dry,

caryatid

I used to read The Baby-sitters Club a lot. Shameful thing, I know. I remember reading one chapter where the girl recalls how she could not wait for her thirteenth birthday. She would finally be a teenager and wouldn't it be lovely 'cause she would have all these new responsibilities. And all birthdays are like that, until you turn twenty-one. I'm waiting to turn fifteen so I can get a permit. I'm waiting to turn sixteen so I can get my license. I'm waiting to turn eighteen so I can fuck legally and leave home. I'm waiting to turn twenty-one so I can have a glass of red wine with Linux Shoe. And then. I'll wish I was thirteen, when I didn't have to worry about having a job or car payments or going to college. I won't care about my car or the boyfriend I can fuck meaninglessly. I'll just want to be thirteen again.

7.20

I'm eighteen inches away from the bed we used to sit in. I can touch the stereo that plays our noise. I can breathe in his jacket. I can read the words I wrote when I met him. I can touch the playing cards he fucked for me. I can read his words on this seventeen-inch screen. He's twenty-thousand miles away. I can't touch him. I can't touch him.

7.21

cracked coffee-cream lips,

Case Boy and Wonka Boy quarrel and I cover my ears with my hands. They play video games like it's war and maybe it is.

"The computer's screwed up!"

"Well, then why did it say I won?"

"You didn't win."

"Yes, I did."

Curry and I are going to go downtown to give my manuscript to Greasy Buddy Holly. Curry asked why he should go all the way downtown with me. I told him I'd "make it worth his while." Why am I such a slut? Why do I fuck with his mind? Simply because I can. Because I know I have that kind of power over him. I'm so fucking manipulative around him and I hate it. I'm the worst person when I'm around Curry, Wonka Boy, and Case Boy (in that order). I hate the way I act. I hate how mean I am. I hate how I use them.

Make me good again, Linux. Make me beautiful. I'm wilting without you

losing all her petals,

caryatid

7.22

cracked coffee-cream lips,

I vow not to write about love, not to be another cliché, not to say words that don't have any meaning left. I seem to be doomed for failure. Sometimes every word I write is "love" but the letters are rearranged, the sounds are different. All the words are red. All the words are scrawled in blood. All the words are written on my bare chest. I can't help it.

When I truly need something, I've always had it. To have my heart broken. For someone to love me again. To find passion again. These things are given to me when I need them. And I don't need them bad enough, right now.

But it feels like I do. It feels like. I do.

needing,

caryatid

7.23

cracked coffee-cream lips,

I've resolved to stop writing about love I don't have and pain I want to feel. I'll write about nice, safe things, like my hair, my VW bug, my cavities.

I want to sell dork-rawk to the masses. I want to see girls with messy pigtails and black glasses jumping up and down in their DIY attire holding "I love Rivers" signs. I want the Weezer video on MTV every day. Oh, yes. Let's make them the next 'NSYNC. I want Mattel to make a Rivers Ken doll. I want posters. I want t-shirts. I want his autograph on my boob. YES! I want it all!

simple pages on my mind,

caryatid

cracked coffee-cream lips,

The manuscript is in Greasy Buddy Holly's hands. I like saying never because I know it's a lie.

I love smiling at people. It always messes with their minds. And after they've stared at me for a few seconds, they're forced to return that tight-lipped averting-their-eyes smile. It's beautiful. My mother would tell me not to smile, that I'm only asking for trouble.

Do me a favor. Smile at someone you don't know today. It will fuck with their mind.

glory wasted,

caryatid

7.25

One: My eyes change colors (sometimes green, sometimes blue).

Two: I was born at 4:11 A.M., July 25, 1986.

Three: I don't want to have kids.

Four: When I was little, my dad built me a playhouse. I had one of those little fake plastic kitchen things in there. One night I took my sleeping bag out there because I wanted to pretend that I ran away to scare my parents. Of course, I forgot about the sleeping bag and it just got rained on and ruined.

Five: I haven't had a girl best friend since I was nine.

Six: My fifth-grade teacher wouldn't take my class to the computer lab because she "didn't like" computers and thought they were "useless" and "frustrating."

Seven: I'm in love with a boy named Linux.

Eight: I have a thing for penguins.

Nine: I've never smoked pot.

Ten: I have a piece of quartz, a smooth black stone, a seashell, a mini-Buddha, and a rainbow-pastel beanie dog sitting on top of my monitor.

Eleven: I have a Rider-Waite tarot deck.

Twelve: I had Dumbo the elephant painted on my bedroom wall when I was little.

Thirteen: My parents painted a giant rainbow on a blue background with white clouds on my bedroom wall. According to them, the colors in the rainbow are: purple, pink, green, yellow, red. Yes, in that order.

Fourteen: I'm scared of growing up.

Fifteen: Today is my birthday and I am fifteen years old and I wish that were a lie.

✦✦

cracked coffee-cream lips,

I went over to Cherry's, picked up my presents. I got some little candy things, a rainbow ring, a rainbow heart key chain, fake glasses, and a denim book cover with a rainbow embroidered on the front. Have I mentioned how much I love that girl?

Came home, brother yelled at me for not cleaning the kitchen the right way. He made my cake batter and rubbed the spoon in my hair.

Parents woke me up at 8 A.M. to open my birthday card. It was blank inside, so they wrote "Happy 15th birthday. Be a rebel, always. Love Mom & Dad." Of course, the $50 was nice too.

I'm not afraid,

caryatid

7.28

cracked coffee-cream lips,

I always know exactly when Vegan Grrl is going to show up. She said 6:20-ish. I sat in my living room, hair pulled tight in thirty small braids, watching CNN and waiting for her at 6:35. She showed up a few moments later in her dirty, seat-covers-peeling, dashboard-missing 1968 Dodge. We piled into a teacher's van at the school and drove to the coast. I enjoyed listening to Nirvana, hearing Goose talk about his current "girl situation," and reading aloud from George Carlin's *Napalm & Silly Putty*. Girls love Goose. Goose loves girls who hurt him. Goose loves being hurt. Goose keeps going back to the same girl over and over again, even though he knows she's trouble. Maybe I exaggerate. But is it possible to exaggerate when it comes to teenage love?

I think I'm burned out on field-trip-type places like museums, aquariums, and zoos. We watched the sea otters get fed and we vandalized exhibits. Well, I suppose vandalize isn't the right word. The current exhibit at the aquarium is the "Great White Mystery." Filing cabinets were set up as part of the props for the exhibit. Goose pulled open all the drawers and looked inside. He was a bit vexed when he couldn't open one drawer because it was screwed shut. So he whipped out his Swiss army knife (complete with Phillips-head screwdriver) and unscrewed the drawer. I got to keep the screw and he got to look inside the empty drawer.

I hate gift shops. Especially gift shops with stupid signs like, "No food, drinks, or backpacks in store." Especially gift shops that won't hold your bag behind the counter. Especially the teenage dumbfucks who tell you to put your bag in a locker (which costs money) or just leave it on the ground.

After the aquarium, we went to the beach, where we ate lunch. Goose ate peanut butter & jelly & whipped cream sandwiches, chocolate, doughnut holes, etc. Vegan Grrl's sister ate pita bread with alfalfa sprouts. Vegan Grrl ate spaghetti and some sort of rice & beans casserole. I stuck with plain peanut butter & jelly, an apple, and lemonade. You know the sad part? I packed my own lunch.

On the ride home I watched Goose give a girl a back rub, massage Vegan Grrl's head, and do more random cuddly things to girls who obviously deserved it more than I did. Not like I particularly want Goose's affection. I tried to figure out why he was throwing himself at a girl who was wearing (most likely size zero) jeans and a teeny red tube top. She kept pulling it up and readjusting her barely A-cup breasts. Goose bit her shoulder, "fixed her bra," and squished her back with his hands. I stared out the window.

diving headfirst into saltwater with a thousand wounds,

caryatid

7.30

To my Linux, my penguin shoe, my cracked coffee-cream lips,

Happy birthday, you Bukowski boy, you Mascagni fucker, you Tosca lover.

There's a lot I want to say. And a lot of things I want to give you. But all I've got is me, my words, and my stupid gifts that turn to dust in your hands.

My beautiful, beautiful Linux. You're gorgeous. You're fantastic. You crucify my hands, make the petals bleed, make me write words with the blood.

There are no good words for you. None.

My beautiful fantastic motherfucking cocksucking brilliant queer. My fag. My Linux.

Happy birthday, my Linux Shoe.

Come home soon.

missing you like shoes miss socks,

caryatid

✦✦

cracked coffee-cream lips,

It's raining again today. I turn my music up so loud that I can't hear the raindrops splattering against the flowers outside my window.

1 A.M. phone call from Curry: "Zoe? I'm fuckin' drunk." Apparently he thought it was a good idea to drink vodka & diet Pepsi and tequila & raspberry lemonade all night. By the time he called me, he was sloshed. He wouldn't stop talking. After rambling for a few minutes he'd say, "Uh, what were we talking about?" He admitted how jealous he used to be of you, and how you are "fucking amazing."

He lied to his mother to spend some time with me. We listened to PJ Harvey and I kissed his neck. Salty. Very salty. He said it was because he had been running to get here. I don't know why I kissed him. I have no logical explanation for it. It was impulse, maybe. I did it because I could. I kissed his ear and throat too. As he was standing in my doorway, about to leave, I kissed him on the mouth. It was the first time I've kissed him on the mouth since his fourteenth birthday, I think. It wasn't as terrible as I had imagined, but I didn't feel anything. When I lick my lips, I can still taste the salt from his skin. It's a very pure taste. I wish I could forget it.

I worry that I'm forgetting about you, the way you used to talk, tell me things, hold my hand, let it go. I'm worried that I'm not the girl you left.

I stare in the mirror. I wonder if my lips are still roses. I wonder if my fingertips are still petals. Oh, darling.

only blooming in your sun,
caryatid

7.31

cracked coffee-cream lips,

My head feels like a vase that's been shattered into a thousand pieces and meticulously glued back together. I belong in a museum next to the Mona Lisa and some of Cherry's fuck-rawk-art.

Eve showed up in her chick-car with her chick-music. I admired her collection of beef-jerky wrappers, empty soda cans, clothes, shampoo, papers, and water bottles on the floor of her car. We grabbed some hamburgers and fries, and then headed over to Baskin-Robbins for some ice cream before the movie. When we arrived at the movie theater, we got candy and sodas. So now I sit here with a lovely dull ache in my head from all the sugar.

While sitting in the theater, previews idly rolling by, I suddenly realized that you'll be home in one week.

ONE FUCKING WEEK. Oh, my darling, it's an eternity.

staring at her calendar like the antichrist,
caryatid

8.4

I idly slipped a rubber band around my wrist today. I snapped it once or twice. It felt good. As I was talking (or not talking, rather) with him, I kept snapping it. Harder. Pulling it as far away from my skin as I could, then letting it go. That was six or seven hours ago. I've still got faint red welts on my wrist. It was like I couldn't snap it hard enough. I couldn't make it hurt enough. "Why are you doing that?" he asked.

"Because it feels good."

✦✦

cracked coffee-cream lips,

I slept too late. Didn't make it to the DMV. I suppose I'll go Thursday, after you get home, after we spend Wednesday together, after I buy my rainbow converse sneakers.

I got Thea Hillman's *Depending on the Light* but I haven't started reading it yet. I suppose I should, so that when I meet her I can be really snobby and say, "Wow, it's so great to meet you, I loved your book."

You'll be home on Tuesday. I think June was yesterday, I just finished writing my book, and you were on a plane to Singapore. Next time I open my eyes, you'll be standing in front of me.

pink-lipped,

caryatid

8.5

cracked coffee-cream lips,

On the MAX there is a boy with short dyed-red hair, lots of black eyeliner, and an outfit made from gray material and decorative safety pins sitting in front of us. He crosses his legs. He is clearly gay. I can't stop looking at him. He turns around. "Do you have the time?" 1:30, I tell him. After he turns back around, I feel funny. I realize that my heart is pounding like a jackhammer.

with the funny heart,

caryatid

8.6

cracked coffee-cream lips,

I passed my permit test with 100%. Only took two tries. My picture turned out decent, too.

Greasy Buddy Holly called me today. We've got a title. He loves the book. He just wants to edit some minor things, like sentence clarity and capitalization.

My aunt broke down and bought me a real typewriter for $100. So much for character. So much for history. However, there was a cute boy shelving ink cartridges and two guys were talking and said, "Yeah, Trina can do it, she's not on break yet." And one guy walked over to him and said, "Hey, Trina, can you . . . " My heart fluttered and my weakness for boyish lesbians increased.

switching her radio to some smooth Mascagni,
caryatid

"The experience of pain is reduced, even eliminated, at times when one's attention is diverted elsewhere."
—David G. Myers, *Psychology*

8.8

My letters lose their place when the boy comes home.

His absence was a coma. I look back on it now and most of it seems fuzzy, blurred. I have trouble remembering details and recalling feelings. Everything I felt is gone now that he's home. It's like it never happened. It's like I went to sleep and woke up two months later and he's home. He never left. We can just pick up right where we left off.

And we did. He came over early, wearing dark green shorts and an orange Hawaiian shirt. I looked at him for a long while. I felt like a distant relative, squealing, "Oh how you've grown," and other unnecessary things.

He played the piano as I gathered my things. I looked at the clock. 12:05 P.M. I knocked on my brother's door and told him I was leaving. He grunted and rolled over, falling back asleep.

There was a pretty boy on the MAX wearing paint-splattered green pants, black chuck taylors, and a sheer seventy-something button-up shirt. I watched him intensely. Linux Shoe forced me to remove my sunglasses so he could see my eyes.

After we got off the MAX and began walking toward Powell's, I grabbed his hand and squeezed it hard. I fidgeted. He laughed at me. He told me to stop. He told me I was beautiful (but didn't say it out loud).

"Hello, I have an appointment with Greasy Buddy Holly,

could you page him for me please?" *Yes, you see, I am a movie star, a teen idol, we're going to discuss my manuscript and I am going to be wildly famous.*

"Paging Powell's employee Greasy Buddy Holly. Please dial four-five-one or come to the orange room. You have a visitor."

Greasy Buddy Holly and I sat outside a café. Nervous sips from a soda can as he paged through my makeshift manuscript. He pointed out small errors, like capitalization and sentence clarity. I bit my thumbnail. I watched him eat his sandwich. I watched him look at girls over my shoulder. It didn't take long. He didn't comment on content, other than general statements like, "I love it" and "It's great" and "How many more compliments do you want?" It's never enough! Don't you understand?

Cheese enchiladas at Maya's, then Finnegan's, a large toy store. Linux Shoe was slightly upset when the lady told him to stop playing the miniature piano. "I am trying to be Linus!" he exclaimed.

The MAX ride home was fairly uneventful except for the young man standing outside the MAX stop, across the street, shouting Bible passages at the top of his lungs. He looked very calm.

I turned up Fleming & John as loud as my family could stand it. I crawled into my dark bed. He lay back against me. I breathed in his shoulder, his arm resting over mine on his belly. I closed my eyes and made it last forever. I closed my eyes and knew that when I opened them, he'd still be there.

8.11

    Today at Opal Creek I
    nearly died and I wanted
    to touch you I've got
    a bloody scrape on
    my elbow and numerous
    cuts and bruises all
    over my arms and legs
    I feel great I tell
    you great The throbbing
    headache only adds to the
    pleasure I swam in real water
    and slid down a waterfall
    We ate veggie
    burgers and I almost
    threw up I try to tell myself
    I'd rather be here
    than home I try to tell
    myself I'd rather be here
    than in your arms I
    am a liar.

✦✦

I hold the
regrigerator door open with
my right hand
my left hand
on my cock
ed hip
He gently places
his chin on my
shoulder and whispers
"Orange juice, please."

You ever have one of those dreams where something happens with someone and you feel so strongly about it, but the person doesn't look like how they're supposed to look?

I am living this dream.

I am staring at his face and touching his lips and looking at his arms and hugging his body and wondering and wondering and not knowing when I am going to wake up and if this person exists and I am loving this and I am wanting this and I am needing this but this is not the right person the dream is not perfect and I have not found my answer I am the mathematician with the theoretical solutions and this dream that I am living and the person does not look right.

8.13

Yes, I am a loser geek. I play the trombone. I march eights-and-eights. I mark time. I dress center. And this one time, at band camp, we rehearsed until we won.

The day was dull and sweaty. Things are going downhill and I am riding a tricycle.

8.25

I'm going to be a cripple in a few years. My knees are on fire. My face is burned all to hell and my freckles are exploding. My lips are sunburned too. Feel free to offer to kiss them better.

Linux Shoe and I have been having a marvelous time together. My mother says it makes her uncomfortable to see us cuddling together on my bed. She said I wouldn't do that with one of my girl best friends, would I? And I said, What if I did? You'd be really confused then, wouldn't you? That only frustrated her more. She made a few vague comments about not doing "things" under her nose and deceiving her. I don't know.

Don't worry, some things remain the same. My relationship with Curry is still painful and destructive. I still love Linux Shoe too much. I still try to avoid Case Boy and Wonka Boy.

Oh, and Thea Hillman, the real author, absolutely adores my book.

I don't know if I can learn to write again after all this sameness.

I just want to curl up next to Linux Shoe while he softly hums along with Mozart's "Requiem."

8.26

I worry that I'm losing everything. I worry I've lost my rhythm.

People tell me that I can write and I just shake my head. I don't know what good writing is. I'm no Shakespeare, I'm no Bukowski, I'm no Genet. Those people were great and famous and adored.

I am a high school girl who receives prank phone calls from the obnoxious blond cheerleaders. I am the rainbow-chuck-taylor-wearing-wanna-be-boy. I am the poser-writer with a manuscript. I am the dissident who tapes magazine clippings to her locker in a vain attempt to change the world.

I told you, I'm losing everything. I'm losing them to their bullshit. I'm losing him to his pain. I'm losing me to something I can't even find.

And maybe that's the problem. I can't find it. I can't reach it. I can't quite get there.

Oh, I'm stretching my arm until it hurts. It hurts.

8.27

Justin,

I figured I might as well write you, since you were in one of my dreams. I was at a restaurant or something and you were working behind the counter. Someone called you "Jay-Jay" and then I asked what your name was and you said, "Justin Chin," and I said, "Oh, I'm Zoe, that high school girl who's going to be reading with you in November."

You know, you can't make this shit up.

So hi, nice to meet you.

I'm not quite sure how much you know about me. I turned fifteen in July, it took me two tries to get my driver's permit, the title of my chapbook is *Please Don't Kill the Freshman*, and I'm scared as fuck about the reading in November.

See, at first I was just sort of nervous. And then I started to realize that you and Thea and Beth are REAL authors with a REAL publishing company and REAL awards and accomplishments. And I'm just this high school girl and the only literary award I've ever received was "Best Reading Voice" at my high school poetry slam (which really doesn't mean much when you're going up against a bunch of squeaky adolescents). So I've gone from excited-nervous to slightly intimidated to really freakin' scared. I think I've only brought the anxiety on myself by reading Thea's book and looking at all her accomplishments and seeing her picture and then multiplying it by three.

Oh, yes, it's going to be a fun evening.

I'm probably exaggerating (slightly) but I think you get the idea. And why am I telling you all of this? I'm not sure. It's very early in the morning and you have no idea who I am. I have a habit of doing this sort of thing . . . rambling to strangers. I also adore public transportation. Those two things seem to go together a lot, don't they?

I was just wondering if you had any advice on handling nerves. I'd try booze and pills, but I'm a little young for that. And besides, liver damage doesn't sound too appealing.

Very sincerely,

Zoe aka the high school girl

8.28

This is my screaming year.

I've accepted that next year I'll be stripped of my youth. I'll be forced to get a job, a driver's license, insurance, a bank account, and I'll be a junior. It seems all too soon and I vomit.

They'll send me college brochures and ask for my money because I'm in that all-too-important 16–22 age range. I've got disposable income and interests that change with the hour.

Rape me, baby. Take my money and run.

Send me credit cards and I'll join the army and soon

after that I'll vote and drink too much at college and own a laptop in a little apartment in Seattle.

This is my screaming year.

Sophomores are often the ignored class. We don't need the instruction and guidance that freshmen require, or help deciding on colleges and majors like juniors and seniors.

We can't get parking permits or off-campus passes or early dismissal.

We still have too many required classes and my schedule feels like a fat woman from the seventeenth century, being squeezed into a size six corset, sucking in her breath, turning a soft shade of blue.

I'm going to scream while I still can (be noticed). Next year no one will think it's so special that I have a book or did a reading with a gorgeous lesbian or have a 1971 bug.

I am losing my luster with each passing moment.

Freshmen scream because they are now official high schoolers. Juniors scream because they are practically seniors. Seniors scream because they're leaving and no one cares.

Sophomores turn gray and blend into the cheap metal lockers.

This is my screaming year.

It may be the only one I have left.

8.29

To: Beth Lisick, the Monkey Girl
From: Zoe, the high school girl

YOU.

Are a real writer. And I am a high school sophomore who eats too much sugar before she goes to bed.

I'm not sure how much you've been told about me. I'm the high school girl, the nervous one, the "Best Reading Voice" winner at her high school poetry slam.

Oh, yes, the AWARD-winning high school girl. Did I mention that I won Band Rookie of the Year, too? I'm so special I could VOMIT.

Summer is ending and school is starting and my book will be published soon. My book. That just seems . . . incorrect. Not WRONG, really, just that someone made a typo in their paper. My book. No, no, no, darling, you're thinking of the wrong thing. You don't really have a book.

I still need to pick a pseudonym. Oh the tedious tasks of being a writer.

Me, a writer? Must be another typo.

What did you feel like when your first book was published?

Your first book was probably a REAL book, not a stapled-together chapbook. And you were probably a REAL writer.

Gah. I need to get over this. I'm sick of saying the same thing over and over: I'mnervousI'veneverdonethisbefore IhaveNOideawhatI'mdoingandI'mnotarealwriter.

My name is Zoe and I'm a real writer.

"Hi, Zoe!"

The first step is admitting you're a writer.

I told you I eat too much sugar before I go to bed.

Apparently Justin Chin lives down the street from Thea. He forwarded an e-mail I wrote to him saying how much Thea scares me. That's the last time I tell HIM anything.

Okay, she doesn't scare me. She just . . . intimidates me.

Never mind. She scares me out of my fucking mind.

High school girls aren't supposed to think about things like this. I'm supposed to be eating fat-free yogurt and shaving my legs and shopping at the gap and finding different places on my body to adhere glitter, yes? YES? I'm not supposed to be thinking about pretty lesbians or my chapbook or reading in front of two hundred people or literary critics.

Or sending very long e-mails to people who don't know me.

Do you get nervous before readings? Thea tells me yes, always. Justin tells me to procrastinate.

And what about you, Monkey Girl? I haven't read your book yet. I will soon.

Turning up the volume on her stereo,

Zoe, aka the high school girl (a title she tells herself she is trying to get away from)

9.1
Always a day behind. I'm like a dog with a limp or something.

Cherry finished the cover. I'm going clothes shopping with Case Boy on Monday. Curry told me nice things.

I should be fucking ecstatic.

I take everything for granted.

Linux Shoe's in Las Vegas or Reno or something. . . . Bastard's always leaving me.

I spent $300 on clothes yesterday. When I go clothes shopping now, I just keep taking more into the dressing room until my mother tells me to stop. I don't even look at price tags. Oh. Fashion is such bullshit. But I devour it hungrily, in secret, like a bulimic raiding the refrigerator at two o'clock in the morning.

Today's date is 9.1.1.

I start school in four days. I grow up in 1,057 days.

9.2
Thea,

So, now that Justin forwarded that e-mail to you, you're not speaking to me. I understand COMPLETELY. Don't worry.

Cherry Bitch (Cherry for short) and I went downtown today to show the cover art to Greasy Buddy Holly. "Too busy," he said, referring to the numerous different dictionary definitions, textbook pictures, and yearbook photos cut and pasted onto a small piece of paper. I adore it. Cherry says she'll try again and go for something much simpler.

I picked up Justin's book. Yours is still on my floor.

I start school on Wednesday. I won't be a freshman anymore. I won't even be able to PRETEND. And I'm so very good at pretending things.

I hope you're well.

Sincerely.

✦✦

J—

Thanks to you, Thea isn't speaking to me anymore. Heh. Beth isn't either. You've all been far too quiet.

Then again, I suppose you three actually have LIVES. Imagine that. Really.

I picked up *Bite Hard* today. $8.37. I've only read a little bit of it so far, but I really like "Sold" and "Buffed Fag" and pretty much everything I've read.

I should be reading *Slaughterhouse-Five* for school. But it will be interesting to explain to my English teacher that I didn't have time to read Vonnegut's lovely novel because I was spending my time reading a quality piece of literature about licking butts and fucking granola-eating hippies by a charming Asian man named Justin with too many tattoos.

My best friend was born in Singapore. He lived there till he was three. He spent two months there this summer and nearly killed me.

Sincerely.

9.4

I felt cute yesterday when I wore my dark brown cords and orange baby tee and rainbow shoes and my hair was big and wavy and I pretended I was someone else in another decade and I lay on my bed and read worn paperbacks and listened to Tori and chewed on my fingernails and I wasn't me anymore.

Sometimes I wonder if you take the fact that I love you for granted.

Today is the last day of the world. Tomorrow I start all over again, flailing my arms and whispering secrets.

Don't tell anyone, but I'm scared.

I could give you a nice long list of things that I'm worried about/going to worry about/have worried about. But that wouldn't do anyone any good.

Sometimes I wish I could cut myself up into pieces and tape me back together to make something more beautiful.

Won't you please rearrange me?

9.5

I've always been such a bad liar. My heart gets caught in my throat, just like it always has on the first day of school ever since I was five. I try to pretend that I am different today, that I will not be nervous and stupid. I lace up my rainbow chuck taylors that I pray someone will notice and love me for. No one does.

Soul and backpack shoved into my locker, my first-period teacher is gone on paternity leave. I roll my eyes and mumble something about breeders, skimming over the syllabus with cynical eyes. Driver's ed, first aid, self-esteem. What a joke.

My English teacher secretly wants us to be her cute little kindergarten students and we oblige, smiling toothily as she explains the map on the bulletin board. It is the "journey" we will take together, and our first assignment is a paper about what we will put in our "suitcases."

My second-year Spanish class is hardly intimidating. I grope my memory, trying to recall eighth-grade Spanish. Slurred French vocabulary slips around in my brain.

Curry shares chocolate chip cookies at lunch. He tells me about how security guards pulled him out of class for "inappropriate" pictures on the front of his locker. I tell him it was stupid of him to post them, but even more stupid for them to pull him out of class. I tell him next time they pull him out of class that he should explain how fast he'll have the ACLU in there on their asses.

Math class is social hour and I sit behind Linux Shoe, drawing shapes on his back with my pencil eraser. I don't listen to anything and in a few moments I'm standing outside, waiting for the bus, desperate for someone to notice my rainbow shoes.

9.6

Second full day of school. Band. Advanced chem. Advanced U.S. history. Speech. I am amused and confused, always. Advanced chemistry will be a delightful disaster and my history teacher is a cynical liberal, like me. Jar Guard is gone and the new speech teacher does not understand feng shui. Half the desks in the room face east, the other half face west. It's like some sort of battle when you have to stare at the other half of the class. Not good at all.

My aunt took me to band rehearsal a few hours later.

"When was your first day of school?" she asks. I think for a moment. "Wednesday."

She arches a brow. "You mean yesterday?"

It could have been three weeks ago. I can't feel it.

9.7

I blink hard, staring at the dark ceiling. 5:38 A.M. my clock tells me in red numbers. I force myself to stay awake, very slowly move out of bed and into the bathroom.

After a shower and generic shredded wheat, I walk to the bus stop. It's cold and gray and I glare at the man watering his lawn.

The earth club speaks at the unorganized assembly. I wear my brown corduroys and green shirt. No, I am not a tree hugger; I am a fucking tree. It's hard to cope with 1,700 bovine stares at once.

I slam my locker shut and heave a black burden on my shoulders. It is my life. It is my books. It is my backpack and I am stuffed inside, scratching at the zipper.

◆◆

We waste away hours. I stare at the ceiling and he types idly. I think I've spent too much of my youth staring at my ceiling. It's not even that interesting. Silver butterfly wind chimes, a giant green psychedelic "peace" poster, and some cheesy calendar art. I've also spent too many hours studying the badly painted rainbow on my bedroom wall.

We walk by Disjecta too early, so we keep walking, then turn around at the end of the block. When we come back to the building, there's a woman outside wearing bright red lipstick and a mini–cowboy hat smoking a cigarette.

"Are you here for the reading?"

We nod.

"It's right upstairs."

We pay five dollars to get in and the woman in the low-cut dress and brown cowboy boots asks, "Will you be drinking tonight?" I shake my head. "No, not for another six years, I think." She smiles and draws crooked red hearts on our hands. We're just babies, I tell Linux Shoe. He agrees.

Greasy Buddy Holly walks up with the woman who was smoking a cigarette earlier. He introduces her as his wife and her bright red lipstick spreads wide.

While looking out the second-story window, watching the sun sink into the city, Greasy Buddy Holly nudges my shoulder and says quietly, "Hey, did you see that guy who just left? That was Chuck Palahniuk, the guy who wrote *Fight Club* and . . ." I grin madly and listen. Greasy Buddy Holly can be such a gossipy little boy. I watch Chuck strut down the street to the diner.

Men and women spit on a microphone as they read and tears slide down my face with laughter. Linux and I feel at home but we know we can't stay. We have to wake up in a few hours for band rehearsal. We don't belong in school, in band, we belong together. . . . We shouldn't write poetry or go to readings in old churches or write books. We're just babies, right?

Nothing at school makes me feel interested or passionate or inspired, not the voices and the people in that building. Oh, Linux Shoe, darling, we are just babies and a few more years in a place like that will hurt us or anything else that's beautiful.

9.8
Cheeks and lips sunburned after hours of rehearsal. I return home and sit. What a wonderful feeling. My parents return home from another country. While there, my mother shopped at Wal-Mart. She purchased candy and an electric hair-braider that tangles my hair and hurts my head. She sighs at her forgotten birthday. I kiss her cheek with my sunburned lips. "Happy birthday, Mom."

9.10
Walking home from the bus stop, I pass by a small group of children playing. They look to be around eight years old. A redheaded boy on a bike looks at me and says, "High-schooler, right?"

"Yes," I reply.

I feel defeated. I feel betrayed. I feel like someone I would have hated when I was their age.

9.11
A button fell off my shirt today.

A little green button.

I looked down and noticed a thread sticking out of one of the four little holes. I gently tugged on the thread, then continued pulling it away from my body until the thread completely unraveled. The button fell off my shirt. I cocked my head, peering at it on my scratched desk.

I looked up to the TV and saw the World Trade Center crumble. I saw the Pentagon in flames. I saw people running from ashes and debris.

I looked back down at my little green button, then pulled a thick black sweatshirt over my head to cover the hole the button had left.

9.12

I cried very, very hard today. Gasping, choking sobs that I couldn't talk through. My brother asked me what was wrong, what happened. "I'm just sad," I told him.

I am not right. I am not right.

9.13

I asked the woman with rectangular glasses and chunky black shoes if she would please wear a pillow under her shirt to give her a belly.

I miss Jar Guard.

She isn't the same but she can draw and laugh and she tells me not to be scared of taking art classes.

I miss his rectangular glasses.

She says, "Thanks, I think," and grins when I tell her she's almost as beautiful as Cherry said.

I miss his pin-striped pants.

She is mistaken for a student almost as often as Cherry is mistaken for a teacher.

I miss his silver tin of candy.

She walks by a room quickly, then does a double take and says, "Zoe," and keeps walking.

I miss Jar Guard.

✦✦

My head is a balloon filled with NaClHO gas and the Second Continental Congress and mezzo fortes and rearview mirror checks and vocabulary (such a trite, vapid thing) and *mucho tarea* and systems of equations and dimensional analysis and proper projection and *repaso* and Maycomb County and William Penn and significant figures.

I just need a nice, sharp tack.

9.14

Sometimes I forget what day it is. The numbers don't line up, don't make charts and graphs, don't make weeks and hours.

Everyone wears red, white, and blue and the day is an elongated moment of silence.

Death = patriotism.

A girl quietly hums "America the Beautiful" and I want

to rip her fucking face off. I want to rip the flesh off her bones with my teeth. I want to scratch my nails against her empty mouth.

But I don't. I remain calm.

My mother worries about me. My father worries about me. I must be doing something wrong, something dangerous, to make them worry. I must be a loudmouth dissident who will only harm others and herself.

I haven't said a word. I haven't told them to stop. I haven't killed the girl for singing or screamed at the boy who wants to join the army or challenged the girl who thinks that a war will fix overpopulation.

I just cry, because it's the only thing I know how to do.

"What's wrong, Zoe? What's the matter? Are you okay?"

"I'm just very sad."

9.15

Linux Shoe touches me for sixty-seven seconds and I'm alive again. It's not alive or dead, it's just alive or not-alive, and the majority of the time I feel I am not-alive. I have a grand list of things that make me feel alive and a somewhat smaller list of things that make me feel not-alive. Can I breathe, please? I would like to very much. And I would like to be alive and learn and kiss and touch and have lots of books. But you won't let me. You rip it from my hands and tear my art off the walls and shove me in a box that I am told to think inside of.

I hate sounding like me, like them, like the girls with the bare midriffs and the boys with fake-machismo grins and the girls with the dyed-black hair and eyeliner and the boy in the fishnet stockings and heavy jewelry on his hands and neck.

I'm not them, am I? I'm looking from the outside, I'm looking through some glass, I'm cupping my hands around my eyes to see more clearly, I'm smearing my lipstick on the surface.

Oh, but darling, you tell me, it's a mirror.

9.17

I can't get enough sleep. I despise sleep and how much I crave it, especially in the morning when it's cold and dark and all I can think about is, "I'm alive again," and the homework that will be due a few hours later.

The security guard tells me to go to the vice principal's office for the meeting. She is not in her office and I quickly discover I am meeting with the principal as well. We talk for forty-five minutes and I feel like I have not communicated well. The principal fidgets constantly, outlining shapes on his notepad with his pen, peeling off pieces of plastic from his notepad. The vice principal stares intently as I look at the principal. This doesn't matter, I tell myself, over and over. My mother said the same thing the night before. She said it like she was God and she had thought of it herself and I had never realized it before. I know it won't matter whether or not I put up pictures from magazines in a few years. I know it won't matter whether or not my peers liked me in a few years. But right now, it's where I spend the majority of my time and what I am forced to put my energy into.

It's like fucking a corpse. I am getting very frustrated.

And I am killing myself and watching others die.

When they see me in twenty years, and maybe they recognize me, I hope they just keep walking.

9.18

"It happens to the best of us, dear," she says with an understanding smile, then continues stroking her pencil tip over the paper gently.

I think she's pretty in a lot of ways and I like the art she makes (censored round bodies and combusting skeletons).

She doesn't know my name or what grade I'm in but she has pierced ears and short hair and loosely laced converse shoes.

I fall in love too easily.

I watch her draw and wonder if she'd stroke me like that.

9.23

I talked to Thea Hillman on the phone for thirty-eight minutes. She lives in a studio apartment and has a great voice. I interviewed her for a school assignment.

There isn't enough oxygen in the water I've been breathing.

My chapbook is becoming too real. I need to look at cover art soon.

There are beautiful boys everywhere. Whether they wander around the library or live in Virginia, they're always too far away for me to touch.

Only forty-two days until I can be happy again.

◆◆

Won't you please rearrange me?

rearrangemerearrangemerearrangemerearrangeme

I don't think I'm wrong or the things in my life are wrong and my friends are not wrong. But these things are incorrect. And they must be rearranged.

I must be redone. Take the pieces of me and put them in a different order and SOLVE me.

Rearrange me.

Make me good again, please? I worry I'm one of those quadratic equations that have no real answers because the number under the radical is a negative. And that just doesn't work.

It just doesn't work. There aren't any real answers.

SO REARRANGE ME. MAKE ME BEAUTIFUL LIKE

YOU. MAKE ME GOOD AGAIN.

I like to pretend that if I rearrange the letters of my name or the numbers in my address or the fingers on my hands I'll be better.

But I really can't believe that.

Rearrange me?

Will you please rearrange me?

9.24

Curry says he's sick and he's lost sleep over this and I don't know what to think. I have a very hard time remembering what day it is and what I am supposed to do. I can't see his face. His mouth and his eyes get blurred into someone else's. You know things are bad when you can't even say his name and the words you use are constantly whispered.

Walking home from the MAX station with my Linux Shoe yesterday I screamed for a long time. Breathlessly and angrily and bitterly. A biker with a yellow helmet rode by on the other side of the street. "DO YOU LOVE ME?" I yelled. My throat turned purple. "I LOVE YOU." He looked bewildered and kept riding. He didn't turn around or make gestures with his hands or murmur the words in my ear.

Fifteen years and my motions are not livid, vivid, or fluid. Unfortunate in numerous ways. I think the only necessary conclusion is that we are too beautiful because being not beautiful at all just doesn't make sense. You cannot prove this with geometry or algebra or your favorite sweater. I can't prove it to myself or you.

Won't you please rearrange me and make me right again? I don't understand why my arm isn't attached to my shoulder and I'm not attached to myself or ANYONE at all and that is the worst sort of pain.

I think I've decided not to eat anymore because I am only filling myself with unnecessary products that turn a bright shining gray in my stomach. It becomes more dull with each passing waffle, soda can, and yes, gummi bear. Her favorite is red. Did you know that? I didn't, not until Friday, before I met myself and shook my own cold hand.

I wonder when I will be content with everything and nothing that I have. This is a constant struggle and sometimes only Mr. Gibran makes sense.

The boys have big glasses, read old books, wear clothing and shoes that are purposely not cool. Yes, I'm in love again. I know they are over eighteen and they know I'm under eighteen and I guess they know things will never work out between us or anyone else or the day the music died.

Buddy Holly boys and David Bowie girls and safety pins and rubbing thighs fighting in bathrooms diet cokes eyeliner earrings silver jewelry wifebeaters screaming pain embroidery floss anklets bleached hair nice pants cute boys vs. hot boys whatever arms behind back can I tie them there whatever rearrange me rearrange me rearrange me.

9.25

The worst things in the world are spelled out in three words. Currently the tragedy I am suffering is:

"How are you?"

Forget calculus or advanced history, this is the most difficult test I've ever taken. I don't know how I am because I don't think I know what I am. Not that there was ever much of a difference.

I think I am not okay because I am constantly doing things that do not make me happy. Anyone with a shred of logic would tell me to stop, reevaluate, midlife crisis. But that would simply waste more of my time.

I don't want to be here or do homework or love anyone or try to motivate people when I can't even motivate myself. I'm supposed to be having study hall, work on homework, something worthwhile, and all I can do is whine. This doesn't help me and I hate hate hate hate feeling like I am trying to swallow a bag of oranges or snort lemon juice because I can't figure out my fucking homework or cross anything off my to-do list.

It's so easy to be perfect. Just don't do anything at all. I could be great at nothing if I tried.

9.26

The deep marks I leave on Linux Shoe's hands are not symmetrical. I can't make an even crescent moon with my teeth. He doesn't notice the imperfections. I touch his hand with my fingertips and feel the way I've scarred him.

Pain is pleasure, says the boy with the hickey, halo of fluorescent light blurring the edges of his soft hair and neck.

I thrust his wounded hand into the boy's face. "THIS IS HOW YOU HURT HIM BUT NOT HOW YOU HURT HIM AND THAT IS WHY I HATE YOU!"

He stares at me and I look back evenly, but it is difficult to concentrate on his face because I don't recognize him. The fluorescent light makes his head buzz gently, first to the left, then to the right, and back again.

I can't look away.

"Bite my hand," he says. I position my mouth so my teeth fit into their original grooves and bite a little deeper, until I can taste his insides.

"Mmmmmm," he groans.

9.28

I snap on the cheap latex gloves and wait for the beads of sweat to form on my palms. It doesn't take long.

"Five, six, five, six, seven, eight."

Barefoot girls are swinging flags on the cool linoleum

floor of the cafeteria. I watch for a moment, then thrust my hand into a bright yellow garbage can filled with ketchup, paper, and mold. I pull out styrofoam to recycle. This is earth club and I am such a martyr, my bloody palms blending into ketchup stains.

I do not breathe in through my nose.

"Do you see what you're doing wrong? Try it this way. . . ."

I tie the plastic bags and walk across the hot parking lot. I pull off my gloves, rub my sweaty hands on my pants.

"Low B-flat concert."

Hours later and I'm squeezed into a polyester uniform, looking around at the kids I've known forever and trying to imagine leaving them. My lips buzz loosely into a metal mouthpiece.

"Fight song!"

I loudly fake my way through the song, blasting the few notes I know. My black gloves start to slip off my hands.

"This is bad—we've already got two flags."

I don't know enough about football to be interested, but I watch the scoreboard. I am mostly concerned with the clock and how much time I have until the second quarter is over.

"Is your band ready?"

He yells loudly in a mock voice to motivate us. I move into our uncomfortable pose, arm outstretched, instrument at my side. My eyes focus on the drum major's white gloves.

Tap, tap, ta-ta-ta tap.

We're off the field. The people who were talking when we started performing are still talking and probably did not even notice we were playing. It's okay. They didn't pay to see us, anyway.

"Where do you get the water?"

This boy pays attention to me. I scratch his back and expect him to purr like a cat. We scream loudly in fake Mexican accents and laugh.

"Fight song!"

We lose to a nearby high school by four points. We play happy songs like we won, anyway. I eat nachos while in uniform, even though I'm not supposed to. My tongue burns from the cheese.

"Nobody's fault, nobody's fault but my own."

I fall asleep listening to Beck crooning in my ear. I think of how I am going to hurt tomorrow. I tell my mother to sew the hole in my gloves.

9.30

"Zoe, it's after 11, aren't you supposed to be somewhere?"

Oh, shit.

I groan and roll out of bed, still wearing the same clothes I came home in the night before. As I'm making bunny ears with the laces of my shoes, the doorbell rings.

We ride the MAX to the place I will always, always go.

(My temple, my bookstore, my savior). We are half an hour late. Or right on time. The pictures Greasy Buddy Holly shows us are black-and-white, slutty and gorgeous, painful and pretty. I choose one for the front of my book. My book will be real in a couple weeks. It will cost four dollars. I get thirty free copies to sell to my friends. I can autograph a few of the books in a really cool way, if I choose. I think lipstick-kissing a few select editions might be interesting.

We ride the MAX again to another place I will always, always go. (Another place with books that are free.) I am fifteen minutes late and starving. My fag buys some hamburgers, fries, and sodas. I sneak outside and eat too quickly. A vapid horrid boy whom Linux Shoe and I hate is in the library, gawking at us. This makes me rather angry and I have the urge to snap his neck.

"Tomorrow is October first," my mother says for no particular reason.

Oh, shit.

I have a reading in a month and people will know my NAME in a month and in a month in four weeks in 30 days in a few thousand hours million minutes or seconds, WHAT WILL HAPPEN TO ME.

Suddenly I am very scared.

✦✦

"I love you."

"Can I have some juice?"

"I need you."

"Let me go, please."

"I want you."

"Can I borrow this CD?"

He gives me a kiss for my CD. I wish he would kiss me for nothing. I wipe his saliva off my upper lip with the back of my hand and press my face against my pillow.

From thin air, everything I am doing is wrong. I am taking him for granted. I am expecting love in return. I am expecting him to say everything and mean everything he says. I am not loving the people who love me and I am not finding anyone new to love and I am not beautiful because I take the people I love for granted.

I close my eyes as he leans in and whispers perfectly, "If you say x fast enough, it sounds like sex."

I thought he was going to kiss me.

10.1

At night I tap my fingers idly against my textured wall.

During this time I also: write great speeches, march field shows, take math tests, do chem labs, act in mock trials, and otherwise agonize over the trivial events of my day. While some may call this unhealthy I believe it is greatly productive and a good habit to get into. It will prepare me for my later years when I can't sleep or eat or breathe from lack of night, food, air.

Spots on my wall are becoming bare from my nocturnal tapping.

10.2

Today I flirted with a boy I don't like very much. I played with his class ring, took it off his finger, made it glint under fluorescent lights. It has a large red stone in the middle surrounded by three small fake diamonds and the numbers "2003" engraved in the cheap silver. I still have it. I pretend he's my boyfriend and that he's in love with me. I wonder when he'll want his ring back.

Today I ruined a girl I love very much. I stood in front of a dim room scattered with people and screamed at the top of my lungs, "I hate her!" I said her name, I said where she lived and the things she's done, and by the time I was done, everyone else hated her too. I curled up on the cool tile and sobbed. I moved away from my own body. I wonder if she'll accept my apology.

Today I kissed a boy I need more than anything. His lips were very dry and he wore a baggy tan sweatshirt rolled up to his elbows. I tried to crawl inside of him where it was warm and safe, but I couldn't get that close. I wonder if he would let me wear his sweatshirt so I could smell like him.

I don't want to be tired anymore.

To Thea,

I didn't write a beautiful speech about you. I organized my notes, spoke as well as I could on short notice, but I didn't make anything beautiful about you.

I feel like I've insulted you and my stomach hurts.

I was too busy marching, volunteering, shopping, sleeping, homework-ing, learning chemical formulas, calling bicycle shops, and acting in mock trials to make something beautiful about you. And I feel like I've hurt you.

I wanted to make people love you and make them understand you and make you seem as special as you are to me. And you were nice enough to answer my questions and what did I do? I sat on the floor during lunch and threw together a rather marginal speech about you. I made you seem like anyone else. And they didn't care.

I didn't make them care, Thea.

I got an 86% and I don't care. I feel like I should have gotten an F. Everyone else says, "Gee, Zoe, even your worst speech is better than my best!" And that only makes me more upset. Forgive me, Thea. Please.

10.3

Seventeen hundred students in this school and I walk down the hall behind the one person who makes me homicidal. For no reason at all, seeing the back of his head makes my blood race. Repeated images of his head bashed against the gray lockers and sticky red blood running down the side of his face and matted in his hair. Cheeks and eyes plump with bruises. Holding his sides and groaning and begging for mercy and tears making trails in the blood on his cheeks as I kick him in the ribs over and over. This is what I see.

Will Paul Revere ever stop feeling his hands on his body and will I ever be able to look at the British Boy and not want to kill him?

Blood on my palms, fingers trailing on the wall. Four thick red lines on blue school paint.

My best friend was raped.

10.4

"The defense calls Paul Revere."

But Paul Revere isn't here. And neither am I, Mr. Benjamin Franklin, just another character manipulated for educational purposes.

This is a mock trial. This is pretend. But Paul Revere is real.

I'm quite a few miles away, staring intently at the clock, wondering where he is and whose hand he is holding and if he is playing with his thick silver rings.

He is somewhere in a small room, I imagine, saying the

words *hand* and *penis* repeatedly in different arrangements, telling them his pain.

"He isn't here," I explain to the jury of tenth graders.

In chemistry, the boy who raped Paul Revere is late. I glare. I spit at his feet. I punch him in the stomach.

I want to scream and run out of the room, but I can't. I have to sit there, fifteen feet away from him, wondering if his hands can reach out and touch me.

Touch me the wrong way. Kill me.

I want to rip his throat out. I want to stamp on his toes. I want him to crumble.

I can't.

I can't fix this, fix him, make things better. I can't kiss Paul Revere and ride away with him on his horse.

Paul Revere looks away and I stroke his jaw and throat with the backs of my fingers.

His eyelashes flutter and he whispers, "Thank you."

10.5

Paul Revere
took off his tricorner hat
and a boy
kissed his forehead

unsurprisingly
he screamed
"the British are come—!"

but his mouth was muffled with
fingertips

sometimes I can't count all
the buttons on his coat
or the distance between
Lexington
and Concord

(guns are stored
in my stomach
and lungs)

they are trying to get inside me.
he is trying to warn them.
and I am trying to forget.

✦✦

The door opens gently, interrupting the silent classroom of
greasy boys and girls.

"Paul Revere?"

He quickly closes his book and paces to the door, ignor-
ing the unblinking eyes on his back.

I can't concentrate on formulas or the scent of dry erase
markers.

I hide my fear unsuccessfully.

He returns to his seat with legs that sink into the linoleum like quicksand. A paper trembles between his thin fingers. I watch his chest heave with nervous breaths and fear he may explode. Fear I may kill someone. Fear I may die.

"SUBPOENA."

"SEXUAL OFFENSE IN THE THIRD DEGREE."

"JUVENILE DEPARTMENT OF JUSTICE."

He trembles in his cheap wooden desk.

I shake too but not for the same reason.

I see the boy, the one who is KILLING Paul Revere, walking down the hall. I hold my stomach and nearly fall to the ground. I want to scream at him and push him into a locker and slap his face and KILL HIM.

But I can't. I can't. I can't save you, Paul Revere.

10.6

PAUL REVERE LOVES ME LIKE I WILL BE HERE TOMORROW.

But what about the revolution, Paul? People've been talkin' up a storm and I'm scared.

Later I hold his hand and I hold Linux's hand and we all hold hands together and he pays little attention. He lamely squeezes Linux's hand from time to time with white popsicle-stick fingers.

PAUL REVERE LOVES US LIKE WE'LL BE HERE TOMORROW.

For those ladies and gentlemen who are unfamiliar with the story of Paul Revere, let me relate it to you gently.

The story of Paul Revere is true. Once upon a time, he did love me and he claims he still does.

I LET THE BRITISH KILL PAUL REVERE.

A boy, we'll make him British, killed Paul Revere in bed one night. I see this boy, this British boy, almost every day. And I am constantly reminded that I LET THE BRITISH KILL PAUL REVERE.

Paul Revere doesn't touch me much anymore, not that he ever did. And soon he'll be in a courtroom, on the stand, like a FUCKING criminal, because a British boy killed him.

And Paul Revere refuses to accept his death. And I still love him. And sometimes, late at night, I plan ways to execute the British boy.

10.9

Paul Revere is sitting somewhere, waiting. I wonder if he has been drinking coffee this morning, if his papery white hands are shaking, if he is going to cry.

Paul Revere will not call me, even though I told him to. He is 109 miles away. He is turning the dials below his ears, trying to lose his static.

Oh, Paul Revere, I am praying for you.

10.10

I don't enjoy faculty meetings or hearing my principal stutter like a small retarded child or seeing all my teachers together in one place (they are just humans with babies and jobs).

A freshman girl in my speech class is appalled by my theories about love, marriage, and children. She simply doesn't understand. She does, however, understand the bubbly junior girl who smokes a lot of pot, likes to party, and is probably too smart and friendly for her own good.

I didn't do any homework. I don't have any binders or notes with me. I don't have motivation or interest.

I mouth the lyrics to obscure songs in the hallway. The people who walk by don't wonder what I'm singing or why.

I think this is why I am annoyed: I don't care about this now and I don't think I ever will. You can write what you know, but usually you know what you care about. I don't care about this.

10.11

There are four quarters in high school football games.

Football players.

Cheerleaders.

The band.

Everyone else.

In the first quarter, everyone breathes really hard and wears helmets to protect themselves. Sometimes they slip in the mud and cuss with lots of saliva. Other times they slap each other's butt cheeks and say in a masculine tone, "Nice job, man."

In the second quarter, they ditch most of their clothing but are still dressed alike. They wave shiny things in the air to get everyone's attention and try to do things in unison. Sometimes they grab each other in inappropriate places or throw each other into the air. They always land safely. They don't wear helmets.

In the third quarter, they wear hats with shiny things attached. Their clothing is all the same. They carry shiny things and put them up to their mouths and make loud noises. They do things in rhythm. Often they make noises in the third quarter that affect the second quarter. They pretend to hate everything in the first and second quarter, but pay little attention to the fourth quarter. Sometimes they slip in the mud and have to keep going.

In the fourth quarter, no one looks alike. Sometimes they have blankets. They stand up and yell a lot, or make noises in unison, but nothing is controlled like the first, second, or third quarters. Often they are scattered everywhere but clump together in odd places. Most usually they choose to group together in inconvenient locations. They cuss and spit juicy gobs of saliva on the cement. They smoke cigarettes or joints where the stadium lights don't reach them. They drink coffee or eat nachos. They chase each other in the dark. They film things and save them forever. But, mostly, no one looks alike.

10.14

I can't write. No, no, no, don't try to argue with me. Don't try to tell me that my writing is good or that it makes you feel something or that you like it.

In the end, your voice is not the one I hear. Your voice is not stuck on repeat in my head.

I can't write letters or words or put them into sentences with punctuation. My hand crumbles under the weight of my black bic pen and I forget everything I learned in kindergarten.

I don't know how to move my fingers to create shapes on paper that look like letters, look like sound, look like something good to make you feel.

I was given an English assignment five days ago that I haven't started yet. I was told to describe a significant place.

I can't do this. I can't fake my heart on paper and I can't copy the answers or cheat. There are no bubbles to fill here and everything else is blank, white, pure, empty.

10.18

As of today, I exist. I am immortal. I have an ISBN. This is eternity.

My chapbook.

I laughed and danced in my black fishnets and rainbow shoes. I told him, "Look, look at what I made!" Greasy Buddy Holly gave me a hug in his red plaid sweater. He handed me my books.

These things I've wanted since I met him when I was thirteen.

Hey, guess what I can do?

I can write.

I can make a chapbook.

I can sell myself on Amazon.com.

I can prefer that you buy me from Powell's.

I want to sit on the floor near my book and hug the legs of everyone who touches the pages.

"I made that, I wrote it, you are touching my words."

You are punching me in the stomach. You are reaching in through my belly button and poking at my organs.

Oh, God, do it again.

10.19

I am lying on my bed in my room and Linux Shoe is pressing keys on my typewriter. I peer at him and pretend he is a different boy. I pretend he is not a boy at all, but a man, an older man with eyes that look at me in a different way.

It's easier to play this game when I am wrestling with him on top of my blue blanket and he pins my arms to the bed. It feels better when I am pretending.

"What are you doing?" he asks, slightly out of breath, half glaring at me. I smile and bat my lashes, "Driving you crazy." He rolls his neck to the side and closes his eyes.

I play the game again, digging my fingers into his hip, making him squirm.

He is very thirsty, so we wander into the kitchen with blood rushing back to our brains.

"I want something bad to drink," he says.

I hand him a small bottle of whiskey and watch his Adam's apple bob as he chugs it down. "Sweet Jesus," he sputters. I grin. He leans and presses his mouth on mine, parting my lips a little with his tongue.

I try to play the game and can't.

I can feel his teeth and the warmth and moisture of his lips and the incredible softness of his tongue as it dips into my mouth. I pull away and whisper, "It burns."

I'm not sure if I mean the alcohol or the feeling of his mouth or the fact that he is gay.

I don't pretend anymore.

10.20
"I THINK GOD."

My hand is smeared with ink from his black pen taken from his gray backpack in this yellow school bus.

It is 9:43 P.M. and I am tired.

We have taken third again for the fourth time in a row

and they have taken first again for the fourth time in a row and my uniform bag is dripping beads of sweat.

Or is that blood.

Or dye from my uniform.

The homosexual contingent of the marching band is rapidly expanding and dividing. "I am surrounded by fags!" I exclaim during dinner. They quirk their brows at me and lisp, "So?" I wish it bothered me. I wish it didn't.

"BUILD DESTROY DESTROY ME."

He is like a hyperactive toddler, asking my why and why and why. I close my eyes. I give him answers. He won't sit still. It is 10:19 P.M. and I am very tired.

I dig around in my bag and put my money into my wallet. I sold two books today. I wonder where the bruises are and what part of me they have taken.

"LIGHT IN HER DARK."

I pace around the parking lot, looking for my mom's car. I get more and more frustrated until they show up with a diet 7UP (I asked for Sprite) and I am not allowed to complain.

The next morning I wake up with ink smeared up and down my arms.

10.21
I hate Sundays.

Maybe I am Sunday.

I don't like not getting my homework done and crying because I can't accomplish simple goals or finish simple tasks or "perform to my potential" or make anyone happy at all.

I tell my mother I would like to see a counselor.

I imagine my counselor will assume I am another over-weight teenage girl with self-image problems but instead I will be another teenage girl with self-esteem problems who just doesn't feel good enough about herself because she isn't "perfect."

I got six A's on my progress report and I didn't deserve them. I don't know what I deserve.

My mother starts sentences with, "You don't know . . ." and "You don't understand . . ."

I DON'T KNOW ANYTHING! WHAT EVER GAVE YOU THE IDEA THAT I KNOW A FUCKING THING? I DON'T KNOW A FUCKING THING!

Sometimes it's like I'm screaming on the front lawn and she sends the dog out to pee on my leg.

The last thing I want is to be another student who slips by with a 3.49 who goes to a state school and graduates with a little degree and goes off to a little job and no one ever really knows what happened to her.

I am scared of what will happen to me if I can't start caring or doing something or feeling something. I am scared because maybe feeling like this is my safety and when I move on from here I won't know what to feel. I'll feel okay for once and that will feel so wrong, I will collapse.

I'm not mad at you. I don't hate you.

It's easier to feel that way about myself.

10.23

Techno Boy wouldn't believe me, but I told him anyway.

"I love you," I said. I love a lot of people. Sometimes I don't really understand why but I do because I need them or they need me or we need each other.

His blue eyes are killing me. In the rain, walking to his car, I thought out loud, "I wonder how it tastes." And he said, "What?"

"Your heart," I answered. Like a giant birthday cake and everyone is eating it and smearing it on their fingers and laughing and taking pictures.

And in some way, I love him. I know I do and I know it scares him that I do. He stops his red car filled with empty soda bottles in front of my house and says, "I'll give you a ride home on Thursday, if you want one."

I wish it was Thursday.

10.25

In black and gray French twill, he jogs across the muddy football field.

He looks completely and utterly incorrect. He is an improper fraction sticking out of an algebra equation. He is a misspelled name on a diploma. He is walking down the left side of the hallway.

He slows to a stop in his shiny black shoes and pushes his glasses up the bridge of his nose. He is glimmering under the glare of the stadium lights.

I expect him to pause in the middle of the field and calmly recite some poetry.

He does not do this.

He jogs a little more and the rhythm of his feet makes me want to be the ground.

10.29

I don't care what anyone else says.

I am a girl from a movie made in 1973. I have slightly oily skin and a crooked nose. My best friend is a gay boy who is equally awkward.

We think we are beautiful. We are so beautiful, in fact, we name each other after computer systems, architecture, and countries.

In my 1973 bedroom with posters of 1973 movie stars and rock 'n' roll celebrities, we lie on my bed with frilly pink sheets and talk about things. Mostly boys.

We experiment with drugs and each other. We call each other beautiful and amazing and we say "I love you" with utter conviction.

We kiss. I think he's got the softest tongue and I touch him.

I wonder how bad my breath is and think, "roast beef," or "salami," or "seasoned turkey." He's got a mouth like meat. I want to cut it open with a sharp knife.

This movie was made in 1973, and I am the star, but I've never seen the ending.

10.31

He is exactly six steps away from being a geisha girl.

But let's start with me, since I was the original-sin bitch to begin with. I pull on my fishnets and knee-high boots and rouge my cheeks all to hell. Next is bloodred lipstick and teasing out my thick red hair a few inches from my head. My eyes are dark and shiny with purple eye shadow. I glare seductively into the mirror, hand on my hip, and try not to giggle. The black skirt stops just above my knee, and my ruffled pink tuxedo shirt completes the outfit.

I am asked repeatedly throughout the day if I am a French whore. "No," I say, "just a cheap imitation of Magenta from *The Rocky Horror Picture Show*."

Later, at home, I wait for hours for the gay-sha-boi, touching up my makeup every five minutes. When Linux Shoe arrives, I kiss his lips gingerly, careful not to smear my lipstick.

In the bathroom, I attempt to color the tips of his coarse black hair. None of the drippy purple dye even shows, so we rinse it out and move onto makeup. I rub teal eye shadow and glitter and dark red lipstick on his face. His lashes, like his cock, grow just a little. "How do you feel?" I ask.

"Like someone is making me beautiful," he replies.

He slips his purple angel wings over his shoulders and fastens a black spiked collar around his neck.

He is exactly six steps away from being a geisha girl.

He is exactly zero steps away from being a fawk-ruck boy-muffin. I groan and close my eyes shut tight.

Do gay angels wear French twill?

He does.

✦✦

There is a supermarket like this one in every city in America.

Even in Tulsa, Oklahoma.

It's mostly empty, except for men in flannel shirts buying cases of Bud Light and a few women with tired eyes shuffling up and down the aisles with children bouncing behind them.

I pace the aisles as well, holding my cell phone to my ear.

No one is on the line. I haven't dialed a phone number. In fact, my phone isn't even on.

I pretend like I'm saying something while poking at a package of meat. "Did he really?" I ask, acting really interested as I hold up some chicken legs in the light.

The blood rushes to the bottom of the package.

I sit cross-legged in front of the deli, sausage held to my ear, staring at the children I know.

Today is Halloween and I am in a supermarket. I am fifteen years old. I am dressed as Magenta from *The Rocky Horror Picture Show*.

"Oh really?" asks the sausage.

I nod, digging my teeth into the juicy flesh.

Truth never tasted so good.

11.3

I'm really not going anywhere. I've been on this bus inhaling the aroma of cow manure for hours. I don't remember where I'm going or why. Today isn't happening yet. To me it's still Tuesday. Still July. Linux Shoe is still gone and I'm still alone. But things change. Boys become butterflies that rest gently on my shoulder. Girls become creatures who look out windows tearfully and ask why.

It is today and I am looking out this bus window for the last time, even if I don't want to believe it. Time is a four-letter word. In twenty-four hours I'll be famous for exactly thirteen minutes and hundreds of people will love me. Or at least pretend to, to be polite.

I'm not sure what happens after that. I'm not sure what happened before that, either. Maybe nothing or maybe this strange lithe boy who is swiftly running next to me in purple wings and fairy eye shadow fell in love with me and decided to oblige my request.

I am fifteen and I have a book. No one knows this. They know that I didn't get a good grade on that last assignment and I spend my time in class either reading or listening to music or writing in my notebook. I wondered why I was chosen to be swallowed whole and who else will want to taste me. I wonder if I will really read in Seattle or Border's. I wonder if a crowd of people will come to see just me.

The color of my hair and stockings will undoubtedly amuse everyone who sees me. I am not what they expect. A fifteen-year-old who can write, with a book reading at Powell's. I am not a punk dyke girl or an indian-cotton-wearing hippie. I am Zoe Trope and I am turning to life. I am choosing life. I am watching it rush by outside the window of this yellow school bus.

11.5
This is not the end of anything but the beginning of everything.

My stomach feels shakier now than it did yesterday. People know me and have seen me and my lips and my voice (which did not crack or break). Yesterday did not happen but according to anyone else, it did.

I am now a real person. I stood naked behind a wooden podium and they laughed, not at me, but at my words, which might even imply that I'm funny.

I have a panda wearing a red scarf sitting on my bed. I have a Björk CD in my discman. I'm wearing a shiny white shirt and Linux is hiding a black corset. I would not have happened without everyone else.

A caryatid is not made out of air. Something has to make the caryatid stand.

11.7

How did you do that to me? How did you melt me under the bright stage lights? How did you love me fifteen or thirty-five feet away?

How come you didn't have any questions? I'm sorry if I wasn't interesting enough.

I tried to choose pieces you might enjoy and you seemed to, at least, when I said something, you laughed and I was rather surprised. I didn't even know what to do the first time I heard that sound. I tried to pause, but that seemed snotty so I continued.

Hey, did you love me? What about you, the girl in the glasses who wanted Cherry and Linux to sign your book for your friend Annie?

You kinda made me feel like a movie star, Julia Roberts with smaller lips or Tom Cruise with a bigger cock.

I think you make me beautiful. Thank you.

Love.

11.10

I think I've swallowed a pound of salt. I can feel it settling in the bottom of my stomach, soaking up every drop of liquid in my body. Pretty soon I'll be nothing but a red block of grainy sodium and people will take little pieces of me and sprinkle me on their French fries. My body feels so sour right now I want to puke out everything that's in me, every bad thing that I can taste and not taste but feel, I want it out. I want it out of me. It's slowly turning me black, I can feel it snaking through my veins and coloring my skin.

What rational person would throw their history book at the wall and create a hole with a three-inch diameter?

I am tasting his mouth and looking at him and he is scared. I am staring at my wall curled up in the fetal position and he is scared. I am saying I love you and he is scared.

He asks me why I don't hit him, like that will solve anything. I hit the other boys, kissed the other boys, shunned the other boys, loved the other boys. They still feared me, no matter what I said or did.

I love people too much.

I love people too much and for this reason, I will always be alone.

11.11

Dear Curry,

Hey. I know we talk all the time, but it kinda feels like nothing is ever said. Do you feel that way?

Tonight you called me at 11:27 P.M. and we talked for seventy-four minutes. We never used to talk this late at night, but now we have to because your mother won't let you use the phone, especially when you're talking to me.

Sometimes I wonder what she has against me, but then I remember I'm confident and intelligent and—gasp—fat! These are things she will never, never be. But she doesn't matter, and you will spend the rest of your life trying to convince yourself of that fact.

She doesn't matter.

My mother calls you "psycho boy" when you aren't around. Sometimes that hurts more than any of the things you ever did to me, ever said to me. I can forgive you and forget the things you did, but my mother has trouble forgetting the pain you put me through and how scared I was when you gave me back all our old letters and I thought you were going to kill yourself or someone else.

Now that I think about it, I remember sitting in the counselor's office and I remember telling her all about it and I remember her promising to do something and telling me it would be okay in that funny almost-Texan accent of hers. I remembered how I threw all our old letters into the garbage, right there, in her office.

I should have recycled them.

Sometimes I'm not sure what I want from you or what you want from me. Sometimes I think we are just as lost as we ever were, and we're not finding anything new, we just keep circling the same landmarks because we know what they look like and they are easy to spot on the map.

It's hard when you get so pretty. Hard in different ways. Pretty in different ways. Like when you wear those gray pants and that shirt from Magpie and god if I had a cock I'd get hard just looking at you. It's hard when I think you are pulling away from things only to cling to them days later. When you get pretty when you write things that make me believe that you do know how to breathe without them, me, us.

Sometimes I hate the way you answer questions with lines from movies or songs. I hate the way you are so willing to use someone else's answer instead of your own. I hate the way you try so hard to be vague and obscure and you just make me frustrated.

Sometimes I hate the way I get frustrated at you.

Do you remember when we were thirteen years old and all we did was sit in the storage room and kiss? We were supposed to be working on an independent study project for science. I remember I gave you a hickey and you were so skinny I thought you would snap like a toothpick.

Ever notice how you can't suck liquid through a swizzle stick?

Remember when we told everyone to "fuck off" and if they asked if we were going out, we would answer, "It's just casual sex." So smart, so cool, so aloof.

Nobody asks anymore. They stopped caring.

But hey, I gotta know, *is* it just casual sex?

Or do I say "I love you" for a reason?

Yours.

11.15

Dear Poke,

I loved your concert tonight. Maybe I just love you, but I loved the concert, too. I love the way you fuck your naked guitar with your thick fingers and the way your feet seem caged by your too-small faded converse shoes. Yeah, it was great.

I don't know when you got so tall, but it's fun when I wrap my arms around you and like a giraffe you press your nose into my hair. Sometimes you lick my hair and that's gross, but mostly you just smell it and make noises.

I used to hate you in the seventh grade. I was mad at everything then. You were tall then, too. But you wore khakis and polo shirts and bleached your hair a bright yellow color. You played guitar, but I can't even remember what kind of music came out of it.

I would have liked to take Polaroids of you every day for a year. Then put them together like a flipbook and I could have watched you go from blond to gray to black. I like you in black.

I like you in your high-water polyester pants and shiny black tie. I like your too-long black hair, which you attempt to make stand on end. I love the words you write.

I wanna watch you get more pretty. I wasn't so good at watching before, but I'm watching really closely now. I'm memorizing the way you write your H's and cross your T's so when someone asks me one day, I can tell them exactly how you do it.

Much love.

11.17
Dear Curry,

You have so many veins in your feet. More veins than kisses I've given you in the past two years.

Sometimes I don't look at your face, but I can feel how much it hurts you when you have to leave first from the party, when your parents won't let you stay later, when everyone is there to say good-bye to you.

Dirty monopoly doesn't work as well when there are an odd number of girls and boys and the game depends on the people sitting to your right and left.

"Illinois Avenue."

"What do you have to do for that?"

"That's a hundred and sixty dollars."

"Kiss the person to your right."

"No, I own it, you owe me fourteen dollars."

We tried to play after you left but the girl to my left has a saliva phobia and Wonka Boy is gay. Supposed. He doesn't kiss like he wants boys, but then again, neither does Linux Shoe.

At 7-11 we bought cherry slurpees and I bought a package of tiny little deep-fried cocks, the kind Hostess prefers to call Twinkies.

In another girl's room we played truth or dare for exactly four minutes. I had to kiss this other girl, then kiss my best friend for half a minute. Their tongues were lazy and stupid and thick in my mouth.

(Is it wrong that I like kissing girls but I didn't like kissing her and I want to fall in love with a girl?)

I watched the meteor shower at 2 A.M. I lay on a cold sidewalk in front of a stranger's house. I can't remember who, but as we were lying there someone said, "Just think of how many people are watching the exact same thing right now."

Love you.

11.22

my father falling asleep in the recliner.

pushing my aunt in her wheelchair down the wet sidewalk.

my brother's refusal to eat salad.

the deviled eggs.

joni mitchell on the stereo.

my mother's burned sweet potatoes.

my brother cheating at Canadian monopoly.

rain.

thick chocolate cake.

jack sherry bowling shirt.

annoyed phone call from Paul Revere.

turkey-and-mashed-potato-and-gravy sandwich.

Thanksgiving is not my favorite holiday.

11.23

I like seeing boys kiss. Sometimes boys like to watch girls kiss, but it is not okay for girls to watch boys kiss. Curry refuses to be an exhibitionist of any sort. He kisses Linux Shoe in the rain or in the dark.

11.26

Curry,

You make me so tired. Your dead-fish kisses and white-paper hands make me feel empty.

This is good-bye until I forgive you again tomorrow.

11.27

Curry,

I hope you really loved our kiss today. My tongue in your mouth, tasting your teeth, sucking out your breath.

I hope you really loved it. I hope your fucking eyes were closed. I hope it was the best kiss.

It was the last one.

11.29

Linux Shoe,

Have fun with that girl at the winter formal. I hope she makes you more beautiful than I was ever able to.

I imagine Curry will sit at home with his friends Mr. Jack Daniel's or Mr. Seagram's 7. Maybe a blood vessel in his brain will explode.

Take lots of pictures and tell me all about it.

Much love.

Zoe (who is not jealous at all that you're going to a formal without her or that you don't want to go to the senior prom together because you have the silly notion that some boy will ask you to go with him because really she's just nervous that some boy might really ask YOU but not her)

11.30

I fucked up the brownies.

They wouldn't come out in neat even squares so everyone dug their hands in and ate clumps instead.

Case Boy reminded me to shush every time I said *faggot* or *dick* because his mother was asleep in the next room.

We tried to watch a movie but there was too much talking and not enough interest and the irresponsible use of the blanket Case Boy brought out of his room.

We've got to be a family 'cause we really can't stand each other sometimes.

12.1

I kissed Curry. I said I wasn't going to anymore and even when I wrote that I knew it was kind of a lie. I'm sorry.

Well. Sort of sorry. I'm sorry I lied to you and tried to threaten him because I knew that I could never, ever stop loving him or stop kissing him.

It wasn't just one kiss or a peck on the lips or a small hug.

I really kissed him. It didn't feel bad. I didn't feel like a whore or like he didn't care or like he wasn't even there.

I kissed Paul Revere. Quite a few times. On my bed, while he was standing, holding him, sitting down, in the rain. I didn't kiss him on the MAX or in the mall. I made fun of the way he kept pulling up his fishnet stockings. I asked him if he had to do that in public.

I like rainy afternoons where my room is naturally dark and there are shadows everywhere, between my fingertips and our tongues and my parents never walk by the open door of my bedroom so I can unbutton his shirt and kiss his tummy, make him suck in his breath.

12.2

I don't hate Mondays as much as I hate Sundays.

The last day of the week. The day when I am reminded of everything I haven't done all weekend. The day when I am reminded I can't sleep in too late because I have school the next morning.

Something bad is always coming.

"To understand how two nonpolar molecules can attack each other, remember that the electrons in atoms or molecules are in a state of constant motion."
—John C. Kotz, *Chemistry and Chemical Reactivity*

12.3

Dear Scully,

It's raining hard tonight and I'm thinking about you.

I'm afraid to write more because this might just turn into a love poem.

What did you say? Was it "jesus fuck" or "fuck jesus" when I told you I was starting a letter to you this way? Sometimes my brain starts writing before I have a pen or paper and I really can't help it.

Our conversation was cut short due to my sudden lack of internet connection. I hope you'll forgive me.

I crawled into bed and listened to the rain slapping against my window. I tried to read a story in *Best Bisexual Erotica* but I couldn't concentrate. I kept hearing the rain and thinking of the best way to write this letter. Finally I gave up trying to read and pulled out my notebook. The rain got really quiet then.

I don't have a lamp next to my bed, so I use a flashlight. The batteries just died. Completely dead. So I'm holding my clock up against my notebook, using the red glowing numbers for light.

I hope you appreciate all the effort I'm putting into this. I'm probably going to go blind or something from trying to write in the dark.

But I think it would be worth it.

It kinda scares me, not that this might be a love poem,

but that you're so much like me. Maybe you don't believe that because you think I'm so femmy (I try to tell myself I'm not) and because I am exactly 11,721,600 inches from you (except when you stretch your arms because we *can* make the distance shorter). Sometimes when we talk I feel like I am playing the perfect game of verbal table tennis and the sounds our mouths make greatly resemble the frustrated grunting of the world's most fervent ping-pong players.

I'm sorry about that comment I made about how your voice makes me think of that girl on *South Park*. In all honesty, sometimes your voice doesn't make me think anything. I'm trying so hard to make your voice fit with your face with your hands with the words that leave me helpless.

Maybe I'm just imagining things.

Yeah, I just made up this really cool girl in my head and the way I feel so nervous and excited at the same time are also imagined and the way I am scared I might be your first kiss but want to be your first kiss is also a complete work of fiction.

Because if you were a real girl who lives in Snowkwalmeee and really listens to LPs and really talks in a way I can't get enough of, then . . .

This might just be a love poem.

12.4

The Old Man.

I really believe you were trying to say something this afternoon when you were talking to me in front of Linux and Margot and Poke. I really think you wanted to tell me something.

You came off as being bitter and cruel. You talked about how my "forty-year-old publisher" is a "dweeb" and I don't think that's what you really meant. (He's thirty-four and I have a lot of respect for him.) You patted me on the head and made me feel really little and you made me doubt myself. You talked about how eventually my writing would piss off all my friends and I would be "alone" and "miserable."

You used to be a guy I could talk to and one who I thought liked me but now I think you think (or maybe know) that I'm just another stupid teenager and maybe I'm sorry for not being good enough because you made me doubt myself. You turned into a teacher right in front of me. You went from guy to teacher. You used to talk to me like a person. When did I go from person to someone you have to patronize?

12.5

While walking past some wooden stools, I thought about you while driving my mother's SUV while trying to do homework or talking about potential I thought about you while listening to the rain and how wet the rain is and what your eyelashes must look like with raindrops.

I really want to hold your hand. I'd even hold your hand in front of my mother.

12.6

I don't want to fall in love with Margot but I guess I already have. Her perfect ironed hair got caught in the rain and turned into soft frizzy curls.

Yes, her lips look delicious. They make me want to kiss her.

When Poke tried to steal her peanut-butter-&-jelly-sandwich-on-white-bread and was wrestling with her and I laughed and helped him. I realized we are siblings. Without a doubt I am Poke's sister and Margot's sister. Her sandwich tasted really good. I didn't want the flavor to go away.

12.7

For once I can sort of pin down why I'm thinking about you. See, it's 10:23 A.M. according to my pink Hello Kitty watch and I'm in English class. I just got done reading silently for thirty minutes and I read *Empress of the World* so of course I thought about you. Which made me think about kissing you. In my mind, I've already sucked on your lower lip and pulled away and smiled in that warm-happy-blushing-post-kiss kind of way. When I get home tonight, I'm going to ask my dad when he's going to Seattle.

I was almost afraid to make my bed with him in the room. Like he would be able to see my thoughts about you squished between the sheets. Or smell you on the pillow-case, even though you haven't been here yet (but I've imagined it so hard it might as well be true).

And I asked my dad if he was going to Seattle and could I go with him to see this cool friend of a friend. Well, yeah, he said, but he'd drop me off at 10 A.M. and he'd pick me up at 7 P.M. and would that be a problem? Just the sort of thing my father would say. I resist the urge to squeal with excitement and just nod and say, yeah, that'd be fine. So maybe very soon we can steal road signs and spray paint our names on overpasses.

12.10
Dear Scully,

I know I had a dream about you. Again. I even remember waking up afterward but being too warm and content and happy to open my eyes so I just told myself to remember it. This morning in the shower I tried so hard to recall what I had dreamed but it just wouldn't come back to me. I saw small pictures and moments we haven't had and pieces of my brain flashed warm colors when I thought I had remembered something that hasn't happened yet.

I actually get butterflies in my stomach when I think about you. Not the normal kind of butterflies though. These butterflies beat their wings against my hollow stomach and try to escape out through my throat from my mouth . . . into yours? Sometimes the butterflies move from my stomach to my fingers.

You make me tremble.

12.11

Sitting on my bed, listening to Tori Amos, trying to remember how to find the mole fraction of methanol.

She wears wifebeaters.

Tori Amos is telling me, "Not tonight, Josephine," and I am screaming, "TONIGHT! I want it tonight!"

To find the molality of sugar water, divide moles of solute by kilograms of solvent.

Leashes.

I stretch my arms to my right, to my north, to a city I've never seen.

We can make the distance shorter.

The rain is fucking against my window, God is screaming in my ear, "YOU CAN'T HAVE HER YOU CAN'T HAVE HER YOU CAN'T HAVE HER," and Tori Amos is moaning hard and fast, like she wants to come right through my cheap CD player.

Pushing her up against my rainbow wall.

Molarity equals the number of atoms in my fingertips

divided by the number of times I touch her skin.

I can't concentrate on chemistry. I don't have any of the right answers.

I like the way she sings in my heart.

12.12

When I woke up at 6:11 A.M. I clearly remember staring at my ceiling and saying in my head:

I hate school, but I love Scully.

And that very well may have been the only reason why I got out of bed to go to school to deal with stupid teachers and a boy with white hair who follows me around and a chemistry test I felt good about and maybe failed and not having my homework for speech class or for any class or for getting a C on my advanced U.S. history test.

And after school when I came home and showed my friend her picture and told him she is my dyke fantasy and later when I slept I didn't dream about her but you know that black fuzzy stuff you see in front of your eyes when you're asleep?

She was *in* that, caught between it, sleeping underneath it.

When I woke up, she was there. Her hands and arms and body weren't there, but she was there.

12.13

My mother let me skip school so I could go see *The Nutcracker* with my friends.

The best part was the Snow Queen and King. Well, more specifically, the Snow King. Oh, how I delighted in seeing every muscle in his ass flex beneath his tights. Mmmm.

I am such a faggot.

All bad feelings of guilt and remorse were quickly removed when my beloved Eve saved me. She gave me a cure CD and an "ani-difranco-because-tori-sucks-and-you-just-don't-know-it-yet" CD. We ate animal-free entrees at a little café on Belmont, and then ate ice cream at the mall. Forgive the irony.

We laughed at the mean boys who were skating on the ice rink and the boys trying to sell us unnecessary home accessories. "It slices, it dices, and it even washes your car."

Okay, so I said it to be flirty, but the guy gave me the dirtiest look I've seen in a long while.

Eve said I could kiss her of my own free will but that she wouldn't fuck me 'cause I had a girlfriend. (Why did this make me so happy? Just the way she said it, like she validated the fact that I have a girl?)

12.15

Birthday parties are the result of broken condoms.

I showed up more than fashionably late without a gift.

Sometimes I hate not having enough time or a car or enough motivation to show people that I'm not a complete asshole.

Curry and I talked for a while after I arrived, then we moved onto a less-than-stellar game of double-standard dirty monopoly. ("Girls can kiss girls, but guys can't kiss guys!")

I think things really haven't changed much since sixth grade. No one really wants to kiss or touch each other (we're all too insecure) but we all want to think we're brave enough to do these things.

Yes, we still play truth or dare and sometimes spin the bottle. Kids still groan and gossip about it. No one wants to kiss the fat girl (except the skinny boy and the flirtatious poser-lesbian she dragged under the mistletoe).

Wonka Boy walked me home in the almost-rain. "Good luck," I said, and kissed him on his cherubic cheek.

12.16

I feel thick black balls of marmalade pounding against my skull.

I am falling onto pointy rocks from a high cliff.

I am broken.

I feel heavy.

I feel steel wool scrubbing my lungs clean.

I have calves made of chef boyardee spaghetti.

I am pounding nails into my ear canal.

I have a desperate need for Florence Dykengale.

12.17

Slowly but surely I am losing my voice.

And for once, I mean this literally. I've been breathing like a dying old lady all day (quick raspy desperate breaths interrupted by weak whiny words like a pubescent teenage male).

My fever was so high when I came home this afternoon that my mother wanted to take me to the emergency room. She settled for a humidifier in her room while I slept on her waterbed.

And now I'm not really sleepy but I finished most of my homework and I'm not sure if I'll be able to get through school tomorrow. I have band first thing in the morning and I don't think I can breathe well enough to play my instrument and I have first part and I'm supposed to play loud.

I can barely breathe. Just four more days. I can't do it.

12.18

My mother wanted to take me to the emergency room this morning, but I persuaded her against such a course of action. Instead I went to my doctor, who gave me antibiotics and codeine cough syrup.

I didn't go to school. I just stayed in bed and tried to sleep and felt sorry for myself. I ate all-natural fruit juice popsicles and watched *Fried Green Tomatoes* and *Rain Man*. During the commercial breaks I switched to MTV and watched music videos.

I wish it were Friday.

12.20
We're watching *A Christmas Story* in advanced U.S. history because this is an excellent documentary of post–world war II American consumerism. I adore this movie.

More than a few people asked me if I'm feeling better and I told them yes, barely. Linux Shoe clutched my hand against his belly this morning, my arm resting against his hip. Such a sweet boy. For Christmas my friends received homemade fudge in tupperware containers. They seemed very appreciative.

I wish I had a lamp that wore fishnet stockings.

✦✦

I miss being raw like July. I think heat forced the synapses in my brain to melt together and create a sugary slurpee consistency between my ears and I let you see all of it. But now everyone knows a little bit and puts the picture together but it looks like Picasso or Magritte—something that resembles reality but is not indeed a true reflection of real life. I'm sorry for telling you too much or not enough. If I knew what the truth was, I'd tell you first.

12.25

I wrote "eye heart Scully" on my palm with a black pen last night. I saw it in the shower this morning, and again when I was opening gifts. It looked so peculiar every time I saw it, like I was seeing it for the first time, wondering how it got there, why it hadn't been washed off.

Now your phone number is written on my palm and I'm pretending you wrote it there. I'm pretending we met somewhere interesting, like the library or a bookstore or a coffee shop, and I don't know anything about you. I'm pretending I fell in love with you when I first saw you.

It's not so hard to pretend.

12.26

Wonka Boy spent his unearned Christmas cash on a red bowling shirt and other vintage clothing. We took the MAX to the mall and sucked in our breath to fit inside. People clogged every surface and aisle and more physical contact was made between strangers than a litter of squirming puppies. Wonka Boy is sweet like candy and sugar and spreads his cash on the counter for the things I want. He is lovely and I am sorry and sad for every person who will ever take advantage of him, including me.

12.27

My fingers shook as I dialed her number.

Stupid, huh? My fingers have trembled every time I've

dialed the number of someone I love or think I love ever since I was eleven years old and dialed a boy's phone number for the first time.

But I was walking down the street wearing my big black wool jacket and dark pink gloves praying she'd answer the phone so I'd have someone to talk to as I paced up and down 23rd Avenue, waiting for my aunt to get done with her psychologist appointment.

She has a broken leg, so I acted as her chauffeur today. Rather than wait in the car for an hour, she told me to go pace up and down the yuppiest shopping street in Portland.

Later, in the hospital, which I hated, I drank hot chocolate and read the latest issue of *People* magazine.

I hate hospitals. Dead people walking around everywhere pretending to be alive but knowing they are dying. Don't let me die in a hospital room.

The best part of my day was hearing her voice. Hearing her say, "I love you."

✦✦

Today I wished I could fly an airplane.

No, not so I could fly to her, but so I could write her name in the sky.

Not just her name, though, but her name with the words *I love* in front of it. And then everyone who saw it would know that I loved Scully. My parents would know it and my neighbors would know it and most of the city would know it. And it would be okay for me to love her, to write her name in big marshmallow letters in the sky.

But I haven't learned how to fly a plane yet.

12.30
2:07 A.M.

It's been nine hours since I had five hours with you. It feels like ten years. It feels like ten seconds.

You are in the kitchen getting a soda and you're going to walk through my bedroom door and slide into my bed and rest your head over my heart. We are still in your mother's car and I'm talking too much and you're holding my hand and I can feel your tiny silver rings.

I didn't realize until a few moments ago that my first kiss with you, our first kiss, on a street corner while the light was red, was my first kiss with someone I am in love with. Yeah, I've kissed Linux Shoe, and I'm in love with him, but he's my faggot and it's not the same. I've kissed girls on dares and I've kissed boys to make myself feel good but I've never kissed my girlfriend. Until today.

You kissed me like the world was ending, and it was. For us, at least. In just a few minutes we'd be in separate cars with separate parents heading in separate directions.

2:18 A.M.

Poke was dressed in a nice black suit and Linux was dressed in French twill.

I was dressed in Scully. Couldn't get her off of me, out of me, away from me. I tried to shed her on the people at the party, but Linux Shoe just took most of her. Poke took his red pin that said, "please forgive me for being a man" that I bought at the metro, along with Scully's collar.

I know Linux Shoe was playing the white piano and I was trying to tell him everything that happened. I don't remember anything I said to anyone at the party.

✦✦

I want to be a better person for you. I want to eat organic fruits and vegetables and get better grades and write another book and listen to music and exercise and stop biting my fingernails. I started today with intentions of being the best person in the universe, but I only got seven hours of sleep because I woke up at nine thirty and stared at the ceiling and couldn't fall back asleep. I tried to eat breakfast but I didn't have any appetite and nothing looked good.

I showered and dressed, wearing the same jeans as yesterday, thinking maybe your head would appear in my lap if I could make everything the same as it was. If I wanted it badly enough.

My stomach wouldn't be quiet so I finally gave up and went into the kitchen to get something to eat and opted for the healthy breakfast choice of entenmann's chocolate cake. So much for eating organic. I did, however, eat a tangerine popsicle later, which I managed to convince myself actually counted as a fruit.

I ate dinner very slowly and drank a diet coke and tried to believe that by chewing twenty-six times and pausing between bites and sipping my drink that I would somehow make you love me more.

12.31

In the back of your mother's car when she was pumping gas, I asked to see your hand. I wanted to touch you, but mostly I wanted to see if your hands were shaking as much as mine because they looked like they were because you were playing with them so much.

On the green couch in front of Coffee Messiah, my ass sank into the giant groove and you immediately demanded my hand or you said you would come and kill me in my sleep. I gave you my hand, even though I wished you'd come visit me in my sleep, maybe to kill me or do something less violent.

My favorite thing is to slip a safety pin under my skin,

usually a fingertip, then rip the safety pin off my hand and make the skin break. It doesn't hurt, but it looks ugly. Sometimes I chew on the broken skin.

I keep going back to our western religion. Your neck was pale velvet and I wanted to slide into the spot beneath your ear. I tried to stop breathing and make everything slow down and I wanted to turn my lips into expensive peacock feathers but I couldn't.

The dark upstairs hallway of the Lambert House, you were walking behind me. I put both hands behind my back, palms upward, hoping you would hold one or both of them. It was so dark you couldn't see my lonely fingers.

1.1

I spent the first fifteen minutes of the New Year waiting for the phone ring.

This is the rest of my life: staring at the ceiling, waiting for someone's voice to try to reach me.

1.3

It's not raining tonight.

I've been in love for exactly one month and I know they know. Everyone must know. I wonder if they know I'm gay, if that's what they must think. But I'm not *gay*, I'm just in love and I fell in love with a girl. This makes everything much more difficult. Everyone understands gay, no one understands love.

162

1.4

Sir.

Thanks for the ride home.

I've gotta know, why do you drive twenty miles over the speed limit? I mean, just 'cause the roads are long and dark and out in hick country doesn't give you an excuse to push the pedal of your nice-new-minivan to the floor when you've got three kids and your wife in the car. I'd just like to tell you that water with a fancy name from a thick plastic bottle is not any better than the shit you get from your kitchen sink.

Why do you apply lotion to your hands while driving? Do you WANT to lose the friction between your hands and the steering wheel?

You're an asshole. I hope you really believe all that drippy music you were playing—sugary warm voices telling you things like, "Blessed is the one who follows the path of the Lord" and "The Lord is the way to the light" and you can't see the songs, but they're all a radiant glowing spiritual sort of white. The really clean sort of white, the color that you want your teeth to be, your skin to be, your soul to be. Yeah, well, I hope you really believe that shit 'cause you're going to need it when you drive your precious minivan into a telephone pole or murder your wife or fuck your daughter.

1.5

Conversation with a sexually repressed adolescent male:

"Isn't she hot?" I say, as I hold up the Tori CD.

"You can't see half of her."

I note that half of her face is shadowed, then try to point out the cleavage. "But you only need to see this half of her, anyway."

"Yeah, but you can't see half of her face."

I pick up another CD cover with her face and say, "Here, this is her face. Do you want to come on it?"

"Not really."

"ARE YOU NUMB FROM THE WAIST DOWN?!"

"If I was, I wouldn't be able to walk."

1.9

Chemistry makes me hate myself.

I think there is something wrong in letting a child live fourteen or fifteen years believing that everything is so easy and that she'll really never have to try at anything 'cause she's so naturally talented.

Couldn't you have let me fail at least a few times? Just to know what it felt like?

This isn't even really failure. I got an A on my last lab. But it takes me so long to figure things out, so long for me to understand them. I feel so slow.

I feel like how all the other kids must feel. Some of

them feel this way all the time.

I just feel it for ten or fifteen minutes while struggling through chemical-reaction equations and laboratory procedures. I can't even begin to fathom feeling this way all the time.

Maybe this just makes me extra melancholy 'cause I want her to show up at my door with a daisy bouquet. I need a dyke with slick-backed hair in a vinyl jacket and a heart the size of New Hampshire.

✦✦

Shameless fingers turn on the radio and play your favorite song. I'm in the kitchen with a spatula, sliding over the linoleum floor in my socks, screaming at the top of my lungs. Maybe you're in your kitchen right now and my voice is coming out of your stovetop or cookie jar. I yell louder but my voice isn't distinguishable from the radio and I know that no matter how hard I try, this plastic spatula can't reach you.

1.11
Tonight I was out walking the dog and I started running the last couple of blocks back to my house (not a smart idea when one is wearing a giant black wool coat and a cashmere scarf) and I told myself that if I could run all the way back to my house without stopping that she would be

there. So even though the coat was suffocating me and my lungs were burning I ran up to my front door and swung it open hard. She wasn't there, but I felt like I had justified myself, earned some sort of invisible reward.

When I take tests or do assignments, I decide that if I score below a certain number that she won't love me anymore. If I turn my homework in late, we'll get in a fight. If my shoe comes untied, I'll say something stupid and make her upset.

If I get an A on this next test, she'll come visit. If I finish reading that book I started, she'll love me more. If I write more neatly, she'll hold my hand longer.

1.12

An impatient whine: "Help me with the 'girl'!"

Linux Shoe sighs and positions the temporary word tattoo on my neck and I hold a wet sponge against it. The phrase "i am your rainbow girl" is the end result, a wobbly line of black letters on the side of my throat.

(Later, at Gracie's, a church-turned–hipster convention holds an outrageously scandalous event known as the "Booty Call.")

Poke, Margot, Linux, and I wander in and take a seat on the hard scratchy green pews. A head turns around from the pew in front of us. "Hey, are you the girl who wrote that book about high school?"

I beam and wish I had a better mouth to smile.

I tell her that yes I wrote that book and it's for sale for $5 at the merchandise table and if she buys a copy I'd be happy to sign it. And she says yeah, she'd been looking for it but couldn't remember the title and her roommate teaches high school English and wants to read it.

Then Greasy Buddy Holly introduces me to Jemiah (juh-mee-uh, not juh-my-uh) and she sits down and we talk and she takes a picture of me with her iZone sticky-film camera and sticks it under her armpit ("Heat," she tells me, "makes it develop faster") and she hands me the picture and I can already see myself putting it in an envelope to mail to Scully.

Greasy Buddy Holly reads some geriatric erotica, then a cute dyke reads two short stories about fucking police officers and hair-pulling fetishes, a crazy lady who looks eerily like Cherry demonstrated the use of a light-saber vibrator, Jemiah read some very lovely vampire stuff from *Wounds*, and, perhaps most memorably, a writer named Jason who was very drunk slurred his way through a very loud and emotional excerpt from his new book. Earlier in the evening he had plopped down next to my friends and calmly stated, "I am the best gay-boy reader ever."

I think he fucked a girl in the bathroom.

Greasy Buddy Holly ended up in a bunny suit on the floor with a nameless man.

Afterward, loud hip-hop music blaring, I stood with a very tired-looking Margot. She says she's mad that I kept covering her eyes during the dirty parts of the reading. "Margot, you're too young to see this!" (Even though she turned sixteen today.) I try to apologize and she replies, "Why do people always think I can't handle that kind of stuff?"

I struggle to muster up the courage to ask her for a kiss, some way to prove that she really is as daring as she thinks she is. I don't ask though, I just stare at her lips and sigh. She has the most beautiful lips and all the boys who have kissed them didn't deserve them. I'm sure of it.

My father picks us up at exactly 11:34 and on the ride home I lay my hand palm-up on the seat between me and Margot and ask, "Hey, Margot? Wanna hold my hand?"

"Sure, Zoe," she says, and does.

1.14

My mother spent nearly $160 on shoes for me today. A pair of pink converse low-tops and black doc martens.

She doesn't know that Scully wrote on my rainbow shoes. She doesn't know that I only want doc martens because Scully insisted I buy a pair. She doesn't know that I'm in love with a girl named Scully.

Maybe she does know and she just isn't telling me. Maybe when she said she thinks I'm really intense and doesn't want to see me get my heart broken, she meant that

I shouldn't fall in love with people who aren't real. People who live far away.

I want to scream in her face sometimes. And sometimes I know exactly what I'd say.

"She's real, Mom. I didn't make her up or imagine her. I met her because of a real author because of a real book I wrote and I got to know her through e-mails and phone calls and the internet and I fell in love with her the fucking second I saw her in that stupid parking lot in Bellevue."

I don't say this. I don't utter a word. I just keep a picture of her in my backpack and her letters and wifebeater in my closet and her music in my CD player and her heart in my pocket.

1.17

Finals are next week. And you'd think it was the end of the world if you heard the way everyone talks about it: "Oh my gosh, I have an 89.7% and I need to get an A!" or "I have 93% but I could be doing so much better but I fall asleep at night because I'm so exhausted from studying." Hysterical ramblings about grades and tests and subjects and percentages. Equations are worked out on scrap pieces of paper, what percentage on this test to turn in my homework and flunk the final and I still won't have an A! I turn my head away, bite my tongue, I want to yell at them for being petty.

An ignorant boy in my speech class makes worthless

comments: "We bomb them and then send money to help them build new houses." Or "I don't want to pay money for them to live but I'll pay for them to die. And, y'know, it costs more money to keep prisoners in jail than it does to just kill them."

After my speech about McDonald's: "What are you suggesting we do? You have to have packaging for hamburgers! And you can't just shut down McDonald's. Millions of people will lose their jobs." I thought this was frustrating, since the point of the speeches had all been perfect counterpoints to his comments. Like he hadn't even been listening. During a girl's speech about death penalty, she stressed the fact that the innocent were often put to death. And yet he said that they should all die. She also stressed that almost all of the people on death row were ethnic minorities.

"You know, I think you take three things for granted. Being white, being middle-class, and being male. It's an easy ride for you."

"What are you talking about, Zoe? I'm not middle-class. I buy all my own stuff. You don't know shit, Zoe, just shut the fuck up." I shook my head sadly. My words are rearranged, letters misplaced. He never hears what I say.

The ring of the girl I love is around my neck and my collar is around her neck and I know what her neck tastes like and I've touched it with my hands. I feel like if I put my ear against my floor, I could hear the vibrations of her voice.

1.20

"Are you okay? Are you okay? Call 911!"

Airway, breathing, circulation. CPR tests are easy and I pray that I will never have to save someone like that.

My mother refuses to learn CPR because she's afraid that she'll do it wrong and kill someone.

A bad Hallmark video plays and half the kids leave to wander the halls. I note that Mercedes Ruehl does not look at all Native American and continue working on math homework. Quadratic equations make me more emotional than her acting, anyway.

My Spanish teacher confesses to reading my book and enjoying it and he even tells me that I have talent. I nervously rub the sole of my rubber sneaker against the ground and nod. How many teachers know?

✦✦

Driving through the wet streets of Portland, I reach over and turn on the classical radio station.

My mother quirks a brow. "Why are we listening to elevator music?"

"It's Sunday," I reply.

"Yeah," my father says, "you always listen to elevator music on Sundays. Didn't you know that?"

1.21
Half-nervous, wondering how the hell I'm going to recognize the associate editor of an award-winning alternative-press magazine.

"Fuck it," I say, "I really have to pee. I'll be back in a minute." I take a convoluted path up to the third floor, and as I push open the door to the bathroom I hear: "Zoe?" I spin around and see Greasy Buddy Holly with an armful of books and a smirk.

When I return to the café, a woman with short dark hair in a puffy black jacket is looking around, readjusting her backpack. "Sorry to interrupt," she says timidly, "but would your name be Zoe?" I smile and reply, "Would your name be Leah?" Linux Shoe excuses himself to wander around, but before he even stands up, Greasy Buddy Holly walks over too. I call him a pervert for trying to pick up chicks outside the girls bathroom and he laughs. We make idle conversation, then Greasy Buddy Holly and Linux leave. The photographer appears (her name is also Leah) and the two Leahs discuss photo possibilities. They don't want to show my face, but they don't have any masks or sunglasses, so they decide to take pictures of me with my book over my face. I choose my favorite cover of my book and go with the photographer to the small press corner of Powell's. She fiddles with her camera for a couple of minutes, screwing on pieces and adjusting the flash. I stand in front of a ceiling-high shelf of books, holding my book in front of my face. Her hands gently tilt my arms and head ever so slightly, then she begins clicking. A few people give us curious looks as they walk by. I can't see what she's doing with the camera because the book is in front of my face, so I try not to fidget and realize that I must look very unnatural. I feel unnatural. I smile behind the book, putting a hand on my hip and cocking my head. "That's good," she says, snapping a few more shots from as many angles as she can get.

When we're done, my fingers are tingling with numbness from holding the book for so long. I return to the small table in the café to find associate-editor-Leah staring out the window at the dark wet street. She talks with photographer-Leah for a moment, discussing prints and sheets and other terms that sound vaguely familiar. I sip the sour melted ice at the bottom of my pepsi. Photographer-Leah gives me a smile, tells me it was nice to meet me, and hurries off. Associate-editor-Leah flips the pages in her small notebook and I try to read her upside-down scrawled handwriting.

She begins asking me questions and I concentrate on talking to her bowed head as she scribbles my answers. I don't look at her hands or the words she's writing. It'd feel too much like eavesdropping on her mind or something. I also notice the contrast of her black-and-white polka-dotted jacket and green blouse with a diamond pattern. I can't make out the pin on her lapel, but I think there are red cheerleaders on it.

Near the end of our conversation, a woman (who was sitting behind me, I think) comes over and smiles. "What's the title of your book? I'd like to buy a copy." I pick up one of the copies off the table and show it to her, slightly flustered and blushing. "Uh, *Please Don't Kill the Freshman*. It's in the blue room, small press." She nods, gives me some other compliment I forget now ("Congratulations," maybe?), and walks away. Leah grins.

I pick up a copy of *Nervy Girl!* on the way out. As I push open the heavy doors, I clutch the magazine and books close to my chest, under my jacket, to keep them out of the rain.

Besides, I always feel safer when I've got words against my heart.

1.23

There was this awful movie on Showtime called *Jeffrey* about a gay man who tries to become celibate but it doesn't work because a) he's addicted to sex and b) he falls in love with an HIV-positive bartender named Steve. The actor who plays Jean-Luc Picard on *Star Trek* was Jeffrey's very swishy and very rich friend, who also happens to have an HIV-positive lover.

I wondered what it would be like to be so in love with someone who had a terminal disease. But really we're all just suffering from our own terminal disease. There's no date set on when, but we're all going to die or lose the people we love one way or another.

He tells me he quarrels with his lover about misspelled words and we play games of who-loves-more-than-who-well-I-love-you-so-much-I-hate-you and it's all so tiring. I just wish I didn't take everything for granted and that I could appreciate everyone more and I try so hard but it still doesn't seem to be enough.

"Those who aren't busy being born are busy dying." Wasn't it Bob Dylan who said that? Or something like that? And I agree. The only difference between me and the guy with AIDS is his virus has a name and a ribbon.

Mine's got me.

1.24

Someone says, "Hey, just two more finals tomorrow, and then we're done!"

And I'll be able to say that in two years and it will be too real.

Leaving here.

I don't want to get all nostalgic and please-don't-kill-the-freshman-y because I want to believe that I've moved past that.

But sometimes I feel like I am walking through marmalade. And someone is trying to make me slow down and look at things.

I only have two more years of finals and test taking and frantic study sessions in the halls and what-was-on-the-test and how'd-you-do and was-it-easy and my-parents-are-gonna-kill-me.

Maybe I'll miss it. Maybe I'll miss everything about that place.

Wouldn't it be like me to be the only angry teenage dissident who actually missed high school?

1.25

"You can't talk to her about anything."

And she's partly right. I can't really explain why, but bitterly intelligent females fussing over their grades really irritate me.

It shouldn't. I shouldn't let it. But it really does. It's nothing against them personally, but if I hear one more girl whine about how stupid she is and how she could do better and how she needs to get an A, I'll probably tell her to just get an eating disorder or other form of self-hatred to round out the deal.

Everyone hates themselves in one way or another. Some people can readily admit it and lavish in it. Others just pore over their calculators, trying to figure out their grades, biting their lips and sighing at their 89.9% that will keep them from their lifelong dream of Harvard or Yale.

Because anything less than perfection just isn't worth it. Like academic anorexics or something.

The only amusing speeches are about belly buttons, toilet paper, and germs. I give my reading near the end, trying to engage at least a couple of the students in my small audience, but no one really listens. I see Linux Shoe mouth the words like a kid silently singing along to his favorite song.

At 11:35 A.M. the bell rings and I am officially done with 1.5 years of high school.

I never thought it would come to this.

1.26

My hair curls exactly the way I like it on days when no one else is around to see it.

I move between my bed and computer sluggishly, reading and downloading music and making sparse conversation. Cherry invites me to go see *Amélie* at the Koin, where her boyfriend works, and I decline politely. I'd rather stay at home with my perfectly messy curls and lesbian Lolita fiction and too-loud music.

✦✦

Wanna know my favorite dream about her? Showing up at my doorstep in the rain with tears streaming down her face.

Isn't that morbid?

I want her to need me to save her.

1.28

Today is their three-month anniversary. We go to Fred Meyer to find some sort of gift for her. Techno Boy pulls a giant stuffed tiger from the top shelf of a toy aisle and grins. "What do you think of this?"

"Adorable. If someone bought that for me, I'd marry them."

He glances at the $99.99 price tag, grimaces, and heaves the tiger over his head like a weightlifter. I help him push it back onto the shelf.

He settles for a reasonably sized purple teddy bear and a box of chocolate cherries (a subtle hint, I inform him). I hand him another box of chocolate cherries and say, "One for me, too."

Sometimes I am amazed at the friends I have who are boys. I never thought I'd be popular or good with boys. From early on, I accepted the fact that I simply could not relate to them.

Now they drive me home, hug me in the hallway, buy candy for me, pay for my sodas, have dreams about me where I have no legs, ask me about my girlfriend, greet me with an enthusiastic: "Zee!" Some of them even love me.

1.29

All day long I kept checking the clock, thinking to myself, "At this time exactly a month ago I was: pushing eighty mph so I could get there faster, hugging her in that parking lot in Bellevue, holding her hand in her mother's car, sitting with her in front of U.S. Bank, getting our pictures taken in the Lambert House, kissing her on the street corner."

6:54 P.M. At this time a month ago I was staring out the car window, openmouthed in awe. Thinking of her.

I wonder if, like learning how to ride a bike, kissing is something you can't forget.

2.1

He asked me how I knew when I was gay, did I just figure it out? *Was* I gay? Bi?

And I answered, "I'm in love."

✦

Linux Shoe and I flip through the gay magazines in Borders like it's some sort of masochistic hobby.

He points at the pretty pictures of skinny white boys in tight t-shirts with perfect pouty lips and hard jaws and defined cheekbones and rainbow necklaces around their throats and says, "That's all I've got, Zoe. That's all I am."

I don't think he belongs in those pictures with them. He's not tall enough, doesn't look good in wifebeaters, doesn't want a bleached-blond jock boyfriend. Doesn't want to be in that magazine in their version of the world it's supposed to be.

I flip through the dyke magazines and look at the pictures of the girls who look like boys and try to figure out why the girl in suspenders and trousers makes me bite the lip in my brain. I realize I will never have enough earrings or tattoos or piercings or hatred for men to be a good lesbian. Won't own the right motorcycle or wear enough leather or cut my hair short enough.

I feel like I want to be part of a club that I'm not qualified for, not allowed to join. The coolest tree house with a "no femmes allowed" sign scrawled on the door in ugly black marker.

The birkenstocks and doc martens on my feet don't hide my too-long hair or the closed-up holes in my ears.

I put the magazine on the shelf and hold his hand, thinking that the spaces between his fingers are the only places I belong.

2.3

On the way to the library I gave my books to my mother to hold.

She put all my queer words and authors in her lap and did not look at them.

Sometimes I feel like my whole life is right under her

nose and she doesn't bother to notice. Or maybe she already knows and doesn't care.

If she bothered to look at or read either of those books, maybe she'd have a better idea of who I am and what I feel.

But she lets it settle in her lap as she stares out the window, my anxious hands gripping the steering wheel, slippery foot pressing harder on the gas pedal.

2.9

Sometimes it feels like all I've been saying lately is cotton candy, light fluffy stuff that won't hurt anyone. Words that dissolve and don't mean anything.

I didn't ask for this. I didn't ask to try to be an author and a performer and a high school student and someone's girlfriend or someone's savior. I will never pretend to be burdened by these roles because I'm not.

It feels so difficult sometimes because I think I honestly forget her. Or not that I forget her, but that I remember her in the wrong way. All these inches between us are like coke-bottle glasses and nothing looks right when I see through them.

Sometimes I think I'm just scared to admit that she is everything I want.

In chemistry, the definition of equilibrium is when a reaction occurs at the same forward and reverse rate. I am being thrown forward and backward too often to ever reach equilibrium.

I'm either flying into the air or slamming into the ground, and the person on the other side of the teeter-totter isn't a person at all.

I'm going to get off the fucking teeter-totter and punch the guy on the other side in the mouth.

I'm going to send you his teeth in a little plastic baggie.

◆◆

Tonight Linux Shoe and I went to a cute little Italian place in downtown suburbia (think ritzy-looking storefronts and cheesy twinkling lights on the naked branches of trees).

The tables were covered in paper and a rather tempting tin of crayons next to the salt and pepper shakers. Linux Shoe picked up a crayon and began quickly sketching me.

Secretly or perhaps not-so-secretly I'm envious of his ability to draw. And his ability to be creative and the way he thinks and his relationship with everyone.

Words are terrible. They are boxes and they are not paintbrushes, they are not colors, they are not anything I can use to make anyone feel. I am limited.

Artists can make completely new colors and shapes and designs, and make everything just a little bit different or a little bit strange. Writers are confined to letters and sentences. There are only so many ways to rearrange twenty-six letters. You can put that into a formula. You can make writing a science or a math.

My words don't connect and make sentences or thoughts. Maybe it's the weather. The rain. The rain always leads to trouble.

✦

My brother went on a third date with the same girl. They went ballroom dancing. This is a big accomplishment for him and I'm not allowed to tease.

My mother warned me quite seriously that I am not allowed to make any sort of rude comment whatsoever regarding his very first semiserious relationship with the opposite sex.

Lips curl into a smirk. "At least one of your kids turned out to be a breeder."

This stemmed a rather interesting conversation about my dislike for heterosexuals and traditional marriage. My mother seems to have this idea that I think getting married to a guy and having kids is really awful. She also thinks that I will never want kids, which isn't true either.

I told her I'm not going to marry some guy who knocks me up and buy a minivan and take the kid to McDonald's. She says she did that for us and does that make her a bad parent? I told her no, just different. I don't want what she wanted for us.

She also talked about how she doesn't care if my brother or I date "boys or girls" (she knows she knows she knows) but she just wants us to have relationships. She then asked if I knew about safe sex for all kinds of sex. I started listing off all sorts of embarrassing terms in a rather loud voice: "Dental dams? Spermicide? Diaphragms? LUBRICATION? FLAVORED CONDOMS?!" My mother responded with: "Flavored condoms? Ew. What do you want that for?"

"Sucking dick."

"Could we perhaps say 'fellatio' instead of 'sucking dick'?"

"Fine, fellating a man's penis and testicles sounds yucky. A flavored condom is supposed to make it taste better."

My father: "Tell her to stop! She's YOUR daughter!"

My poor parents. The shit I put them through. It's not fair, I suppose, but they'd be bored otherwise.

I am the reason why I don't want to have kids.

2.10

I sat down to do my chemistry homework, reading diagrams and formulas intensely. Every other word is about her and I am fascinated.

My phone rings. It's Scully. I know it.

I love her but sometimes I hate being in love. I only recently realized that I subconsciously attempt to forget her because vivid memories are the most painful, right? If I don't listen to her music or hear her voice or read her writing, I'm fine. She's a low-pitched humming noise in the base of my spine. Easily ignored. I don't have to think about it. It's just there.

But her voice makes it so much more real. It completely and utterly ruins all of my attempts to forget her. Sometimes I hate myself for that.

I hate myself for a lot of things.

All that ping-pong nonsense I wrote in that first letter? Our conversations being perfectly matched? It was kind of an exaggeration then but now it is the absolute truth. I anticipate the jokes before she makes them and she says the things I'm thinking. She can do this from three hundred miles away and that scares me.

If she is so good so far away, what will she do when she's here? Next to me, on me, inside of me?

2.11

If they wanted my fear, they succeeded. I hate sitting in the halls or in class or anywhere and watching them walk by. Cool, collected, mumbling into the walkie-talkie attached to their shoulder like a pirate's parrot. I only hear pieces of what they say, words like *negative* and *third time* and *in the east hall*.

A little part of me always worries they'll be coming for me. Again. And some days I wish they would. Days when I want to scream or kick their teeth in. Days when I dare them to tell me I'm wrong, I'm too much, I'm breaking all their rules. Other days I'm praying it won't be me because I don't think I can handle their words ever again.

2.12

In speech class today we were researching debate topics on the internet.

I went to msnbc.com and curiously read their "highest alert" coverage. Halfway down the page was a link for "coverage for kids."

Tears gather in my eyes while the page loads.

WHAT IS YOUR DEFINITION OF WAR FOR KIDS? DOT-TO-DOT HIS MISSING LIMBS, MATCH THE FOOD WITH THE STARVING REFUGEE, PUT TOGETHER THE PUZZLE PIECES OF A MOTHER'S BROKEN HEART?

The friendly page showed the cheerful graphic "Coverage for Kids!" with a boy building a snowman and a big cartoon pencil next to the words.

They wonder why I don't watch the news, read the paper anymore. Sometimes it's not just the news, but also the way you want to give it to me. You want it with the American flag waving proudly behind the translucent head of an eagle so I can feel good about killing for peace.

I can feel good about the Enron scandal on page A16 of the newspaper while the winter Olympics makes front page. I can feel good about the profiles of the starving refugees with names I can't pronounce.

WHAT'S YOUR DEFINITION OF WAR FOR KIDS?

WANT ME TO CLIMB THE PLASTIC TANK-SHAPED STRUCTURE IN MY BACKYARD AND PLAY "WAR"?

WANT ME TO MAKE A GUN WITH MY HAND AND KILL MY LITTLE BROTHER?

WANT ME TO SIT WITH MY NOSE AGAINST THE SCREEN WHILE BIG BIRD ADORNS COMBAT BOOTS AND A HELMET AND THEY SING THE NATIONAL ANTHEM WITH KARAOKE-STYLE LIGHT-UP WORDS AT THE BOTTOM?

WHAT'S YOUR DEFINITION OF WAR FOR KIDS?

What's your definition of war for me?

2.13

Diversity Week is diverse if you are white, male, and straight. They lie to me all over my heart and I yell in their faces. Spit lands on their giant glasses and they calmly wipe them clean with a white handkerchief. DO YOU THINK THIS IS OKAY? DO YOU REALLY THINK YOU'D GET AWAY WITH IT? They look at each other, shrug, and give me big smiles. Locker door slams shut fifteen times and I tape my hopeless heart to everything.

2.15

The inevitable defiance of the homophobia of my adminis-tration leads to my mother yanking me out of the closet by my shiny red pigtails. She doesn't really yank, I suppose, she gives them a few curious tugs before finally asking me and then I just step out, shrugging and asking for an ice cream cone.

I told her who I was in love with and she was more concerned with their age and location than their gender. This is my mother and I think I love her.

Flowers are handed to me for Valentine's Day. I breathe in deeply and sneeze all over. I gave up making valentines after grade school. I think my jaded disposition about love and candy set in after the sixth grade. Maybe I don't love anyone less but my hands and heart are just lazier.

2.16

Speech competitions are spilled words on carpeted floors. I curse my tongue and teeth and how everyone from a certain school is better than me. I make finals, sit on my bitten fingernails, and stumble through my story. I am scored, graded, corrected, and commented upon. They write on the back of pink slips of paper but they have no idea who I am and I wish I could sit down and talk with these judges and ask them how much they get paid to judge me and my silly lips. I've got a heart and they can't have it, but they give me a certificate in exchange and I think I accept. I am a whore for attention and I spread my legs as wide as my mouth.

2.17

The definition of best friends is the person with whom you share the most clothing and so now Eve is my best friend and she plays dress-up in my closet and I let her. I give her bags of unwanted clothing and she buys me milk shakes from the diner down the street.

Five days.

✦

My mother ruined my favorite shirt, the one I had planned on wearing during Scully's visit. The agony makes my eyes water. She tried to remind me that Scully hasn't seen my entire wardrobe yet so anything I wear would be "new" to her.

She always knows just what to say to make me feel incredibly lame or sad or stupid.

2.18

Both of my parents know about Scully, but they don't say much about her. My father tiptoes around her name like a land mine.

"He doesn't want to admit that you're a sexual person," my mother explains, like admitting my sexuality just makes him older than he already is.

He's celebrated his forty-third birthday four times.

Four days.

✦✦

Curry leaves a five-word message on my voice mail and I lose all my newly grown fingernails in worry. I call his mother and she is short and rude. Linux Shoe has the same results when he tries to call him.

His mother shoved him into a closet door so hard it broke.

I chew the fingernails I don't even have and pray to the God I don't believe in.

Three days.

2.19

I've been trying to get her attention all year. I have a class in her room, but she isn't the teacher. She spends most of the eighty-seven minutes at her computer, drinking water from her plastic Nalgene bottle, typing furiously, short brown bangs hanging in her eyes. I stare and wonder if anyone else notices. They're too busy filling out verb worksheets to detect my unnatural fascination.

She has a tattoo on the inside of her right ankle. I can't tell what it is because I'm always at least twenty feet away from her.

Two days.

2.20

Tour dates confirmed but I am not a rock star, I am a girl with a book and heart that may possibly be bigger than my big red mouth. The lesbian of my dreams is organizing a tour for me in the gay capital of the world and I can't breathe but it's more than a month away so I can't stop breathing, not literally, at least, not now. I wonder what it will be like to walk down the street next to her and see where she lives. She usually only lives on the page and now she's in an apartment, wearing shoes and her hair dyed a different color than the last time I saw her. No one knows I'm going on tour and I wonder if they could even find this city on a map.

2.21

When I was eleven, I watched a documentary on MTV about different sexual orientations. They interviewed lesbians, gay men, and ONE bisexual Asian girl. I thought, "Jeez, I don't care how I end up as long as I'm not bisexual. That girl is so stupid. How can she be attracted to girls AND boys?"

And here I am, defining myself as PoMoSexual so I don't have to use that hideous ugly word that I've detested before I even knew what I was.

I've always been a smart, outgoing, aggressive girl, which has made me queer in more ways than one. I played soccer when I was six years old and my mother told me that I used to run ahead of all the other kids, holding them back with my arms outstretched on either side of me. Or how every time we played indoor hockey in grade school, I'd "accidentally" hit all my opponents in the shin with my stick (I was a mini Tonya Harding. Some of these kids fell to the ground crying).

I guess things kind of snowballed from there. After all those useless crushes on boys and never being persuaded otherwise, the same sex seemed like the logical option.

When I came out to my mom, I told her it was because she dressed me in pink on a daily basis when I was younger.

2.23
Dear Scully,

It's raining hard tonight and I'm thinking about you. Isn't that how this whole mess started anyway? The second Eve and Maple dropped me off, it began pouring like mad. And it's only gotten louder and more persistent (like the voice in my head saying, "you love her you love her you love her").

Raining like the night I wrote you that letter. But now it's almost three months later and I'm wearing your ring around my bitten throat and thinking of how you breathe when I kiss you.

You scare the fuck out of me. Scare me because maybe you want me and I wonder if it's really me you want or what it is you really want because sometimes it's like I'm inside of you but not close enough inside that I can say all the things I wanna say. Scare me because I don't think you're lying, you aren't making a joke, you aren't gonna laugh it off later. Your hands under my shirt, mouth on my throat, breathing against my skin. This is the only truth you and I know.

I always thought myself to be so strong, the one to push things just a little farther, take another step on the tight wire. You're waiting on the other side, arms folded and smirking, wondering what's taking me so long to get across.

Maybe it's all those secret insecurities I never knew about. All this fear I never knew I had. Or how, deep down inside, I'm scared of loving someone.

The only thing I know is the rain, and the way it sounds and the way it feels and how I think it's going to leave tiny holes in the pavement, it's going to crash into the ground and break it apart.

It's eleven hours until I see you again and I'm so sleepy and all I want is you curled against me under my green flannel blankets.

My teeth are sore.

2.24

I wake up seven hours later with meth-withdrawal eyes staring at the ceiling, fingernails digging into the sheets. Too awake to fall back asleep, too tired to get out of bed. Two queer boys and the only straight one arrive and we hurry to get Scully.

Funny the way that girl hugs me when she sees me. Doesn't matter if it's been six weeks or twelve hours, she hugs me like it's been a lifetime. It feels so good. Scully gives me my PoMoSexuals shirt, which I promptly pull on over my long-sleeved black tee.

Our Chinese lunch sounds like forks clicking against plates. My boys have never been so silent. Maybe it is just because they weren't used to seeing me with Scully or because they are nervous or because they just couldn't think of what to talk about. My fortune cookie says something about an admirer. Case Boy eats sugar straight from the packet and I poke at my sweet and sour shrimp.

We buy vintage clothes, gay earrings, a leash to attach to the collar around her throat, white chalk, bumper stickers, pins, rainbow shoelaces, and fifteen minutes in a sweaty video game arcade. We are picture-perfect examples of teenage consumerism and I don't care. I just like the way everyone looks at us when we walk by, holding hands, or how our mouths touch in public.

A vegan dinner is poked at and we kiss on someone else's couch. After dinner we move to another house, another couch, but our hands and motions and mouths remain the same. She looks up at me with her Cheshire-cat smile and my heart can't take it. I put my cold hands on her stomach and she reminds me to move them higher. Eyes roll and I want to be aloof.

She drags me from the couch to a bedroom I've never been in. T-shirts are peeled off and I know exactly how her breath tastes. I am told later that everyone in the living room goes silent to listen to us. The Cheshire-cat smile is usually followed by the words, "I love you, you know," and I can feel everything in my chest caving in and blooming at the same time.

What's scarier? LOVING HER OR LOSING HER?

Losing her. Losing her. Losing her.

"Words don't always work," she said, lightly pushing me away. A backward step into the hallway, lips smirking.

She grinned, flipping me off as she closed the door.

2.26

We turn off our porch lights and pretend we aren't home. You can never tell what's going on inside because people do things in the dark.

No one sits on their front porch anymore. Everyone stays inside hitting their children and fucking their wives and watching CNN (while not necessarily in that order).

I want to be outside but when I am outside I am driving in my mother's jeep or walking to my front door to come inside to sit inside to stare at my ceiling.

I wonder what people think when they see my house and I wonder how they would feel if they ever came inside.

3.1

Everything seems darker when I'm sitting in front of this glaring monitor. The light stops somewhere between my fingers and my eyes.

I slept soundly in my bed this morning while everyone else did jumping jacks. I arrived at school only to find I had made it just in time for an hour-long assembly, something about let's-all-watch-the-drama-kids-perform-their-state-competition-pieces.

Words were passed on slips of paper and Go's perfect handwriting made me envious. She loves everything in an ugly world and her heart bursts to be empty. She's screaming in a soundproof room and I want to let her out. Maybe she'll open the door and let me in.

Her fingers tangle with mine and I wonder what kind of straight girl would hold hands with a well-known queer.

I wish the light came from things that weren't plugged into the wall.

3.2

I called her a prude and sighed exasperatedly at the sound of her name. I dismissed her as another melodramatic teenager with nothing good to say and now she's calling me wonderful, holding my soft hands and shrieking my name in the hallways.

She says I don't offend her but I used to and now she

likes me. I say it's usually the other way around: someone likes me, then I offend them and they don't like me anymore.

But she is beautiful and I am wonderful and maybe the continued spontaneous use of these adjectives when applied appropriately to the right people can save the world.

3.3

Five Mike's Hard Lemonades are sloshing around in my belly, along with a steak, French fries, and chocolate-caramel ice cream.

Not even a slight buzz. No wobbling or slurred speech. I am such a failure.

I'm scared because June is coming so fast and I'm just standing with my foot stuck in the tracks as the train charges toward me.

Eve and I spend hours downtown and all I can think about is the last time I was there, Scully was with me. She was on a leash and people were staring at us and I could tug her closer for a kiss. It's fourteen weeks till she graduates and nameless days until she's here again.

I'm so tired of the hours bleeding on and the Saturdays turning into Sundays turning into Mondays. I just want to make it all stop, press the "off" button, turn my back.

3.4

"Your hand was so soft. Why's your hand so soft with all those hard words coming out of your mouth?"

Go wants to know and I want to answer.

My hands are soft but heads nod and lips contort and they say YES. SOFT HANDS. I don't think it's my hands. I think it's the way I use them.

Words are the same. My words aren't hard, but it's the way I use them, who I say them to and how they come out, swished around until spewed out like toothpaste.

"It's all about your mouth. Toothpaste words are soft and squishy until I spit them out between my pink lips."

◆◆

I wore my birkenstocks to school today. Feet swinging beneath my desk, they know it's summer, even if no one else does.

Numbers are put next to my name, posted on the doors of teachers who recognize my face. Congratulations on making it into the most difficult band class, good job on the chemistry test, you're the only one who passed that last quiz.

Grandpa glares over his glasses and reminds me that I owe him a few assignments. "I owe you my soul," I offer.

Linux Shoe gets so excited about projects, but he gets too hot and he shuts off. Pulls the plug, jumps into cold water, and tries to drown. He is easily overwhelmed by his own mind and the possibilities he creates.

Most girls make hearts and arrows and initials of the boys they love in the margins of their papers.

I write: DO YOU EVER MISS YOUR HEART? DO YOU EVER MISS YOURSELF?

3.7

If Scully were here, I'd be fucking her.

It's been a week of strange looks, jocks and their boring girlfriends glance nervously over their shoulders at the way my palm squishes against Go's in a friendly embrace. Words bounce back and forth in preparation for a speech competition and I spend my extra time writing a press release for a book tour. I try to decide what outfit to wear to my reading on Monday and Earth Week is going to be a disaster.

Give me some superglue, a roll of duct tape. Anything to make it stick together and hold its shape until I'm done.

Another hour-long meeting with my principal is entirely unproductive. He is hesitant to give us a Gay-Straight Alliance and warns us of backlash. I am tired of his slow lips. I am tired of squeezing my words through my throat, making sure that he will understand and the taxpayers won't pull their funding if I say the wrong thing.

A cute queer substitute smiles at me and I swallow my heart in my throat.

Damn, I really want to fuck her right now. Scully, not the substitute. Maybe both. I don't know. I'm so tired.

3.10

Tomorrow is my reading at Borders. I've always felt this distance between me and the girl who wrote *PDKTF*, but the more and more I reread it, the more and more I see us passing through each other, brief moments where we're together, and then we separate again.

We've been so tired lately.

3.13

Words are strewn around everywhere like confetti, small pieces of colored paper. Nothing that will stay, fodder for a vaccuum cleaner in just a few hours. I pretend it matters. I pretend I am alive and that all the words I say to people will STICK and be REAL. No one listens.

My love for Tupperware increases proportionally with each day. He is my Buddhist lesbian, my writer, my baked beans, my hippie, my groupie, and best of all—he knows about the olive juice game.

I want to write him a letter, but I don't know what to write after the "Dear Tupperware," part.

3.16

I'm supposed to be taking notes on war and hate but I'd much rather love you. 'Cause it's all about love and I don't care about infantry and firebombing because I am outside of it, away from it.

War? What war? If I don't turn on my TV or pick up the newspaper there is NO war. It doesn't exist to me. Isn't it crazy how disconnected we can be from everything else? And maybe that's why I need you, this cosmic connection, tiny piece of some giant puzzle. I have to believe that there are parts of this world that I am still connected to.

MY HEART IS IN WASHINGTON.

MY HEART IS IN MICHIGAN.

There are pieces of me all over this planet and in this planet that I am trying to find but sometimes I worry what will happen when I find all the pieces. When my fingers have to stretch so far to keep everything connected. Maybe my limbs will fall off and I won't exist anymore. But everything that I've touched will stay. Maybe it will be different than it started.

Don't you love my idealism? My hypocrisy? My willingness to sound as loving and naive as possible? At least I know that I don't know anything at all. I can admit it. Can you? Can you look yourself in the mirror in the morning and admit that you are no different from every other bundle of bones on this planet? And maybe the only things that make you different are your hands, the way you touch things, and what happens to them.

✦✦

Press releases mailed off with shiny red bows. I wonder if any of the newspapers in San Francisco will want to do a story on me, splash me all over the front page.

I think my words won't help me with college. I anonymously published a dangerous book about my freshman year of high school. Who cares? How can I prove it's me? "Hi, this is me, Zoe Trope"?

And I said so many horrid things about my teachers. Anyone interested might just assume that I'll trash any school I go to, ruin their reputation, make them ashamed of me. Why couldn't I have written a nice story about nice people? Nice doesn't sell. I'm a capitalistic whore.

✦✦

Did you plan on any of this going this far? Or was it all just pop-tarts to you, sugary breakfast food, cornflakes and orange juice? Was it all about the minivans and the drive-thru windows? Why can't they have it too?

I watched the two-hour special on prime time last night about Rosie O'Donnell and gay parenting and the Florida court case but the parents live here in Portland.

I looked up their name/number/address on the internet. I want to tell them it's love. It's just love. And shouldn't kids go to a family that loves them and takes care of them? A family that choose them like they choose their family?

But I think that's where the decisions end. Beyond that it's just love. I feel like murmuring into a pillow that's smothering their faces and no one wants to listen.

But if I called them right now, what would they say?

"Even a normal healthy person can be injured or seriously hurt by the shock or what happens as a result of it."
—Stephen R. Matt, *Electricity and Basic Electronics*

3.18

About literary agents:

Is this the part where I get so scared that I fuck up? I ruin everything?

I am not me. I did not write a book, I am not responsible, I am not this girl, and I have never been in love. Ever.

◆◆

My name is Zoe Trope and I am fifteen years old. Already I've told you half a lie. My name isn't really Zoe Trope. It's Zoe. I was born in 1986 and my car is twice my age. I can't drive yet and I hate driving stick shifts. Maybe that explains why I'm a lesbian. Kind of a lesbian, at least. I have a girl-friend named Scully who lives in Washington. I met her because of the book I wrote. I wrote a book. No, that isn't a lie or a typo, though sometimes it seems like both of those. Lies and typos. My life is lies and typos. So I wrote a book about my freshman year of high school and that's when everything changed and I split in two. People read the book and loved it and people read the book and demeaned me and people read the book and got scared.

I'm typing this on my correctronix GX 6750 typewriter that my aunt bought me for my fifteenth birthday. I've been alive for fifteen years. Does that scare you? Does it scare you that I've been living for all fifteen of those years and maybe you've only been living for ten of yours? I think I scare a lot of people. I've been scaring people since I was a little girl and I could spell really well and I was loud and I didn't act the way a little girl was supposed to act. I was loud and I climbed trees and I fought with boys. Not much has changed since then.

I feel like I'm lying to you. This isn't how I really sound. This isn't who I really am. I feel like a giant lake, constantly reflecting the mood of the sky above me. I can't feel anything for myself. It's all just a reflection of the world around me or whatever I'm reading or thinking or doing at the moment and whoever or whatever is influencing me at the moment. I am weak and malleable.

When I finish a page, I turn it upside down. I don't wanna see my words when they're out of my body. Like how some people can't stand the sight of their own blood, I can't stand the sight of my own words. I don't wanna look at it.

When I go to Powell's and visit my book, I always open it up and peek inside and expect it to have changed somehow. Like somehow it is growing different copies of itself and it will never be the same when I read it again. But it's always the same. It never changes. I can't change the past. I can't change myself. I am not Zoe Trope. I am Zoe Trope. I am Zoe. Who am I?

Zoe Trope didn't get in trouble at her school for writing about one of her teachers and calling him a pedophile. Zoe did. Zoe is a stupid high school student. Zoe Trope gave a reading at Powell's in front of a hundred or more people and she wasn't very good but she sold the most books. People laughed at her writing and lesbians made out while she read. Zoe Trope is not a lesbian. Zoe Trope is queer. Zoe has a girlfriend. Zoe/Zoe Trope. Which one. Zoe Trope or Zoe, who am I? Am I a high school student am I kissing girls on street corners am I fucking girls on my best friend's bed?

I am not any of this. I am a dream. I am dreaming myself and I am waiting to wake up.

The administration at my school does not like me. I am fifteen years old, I am in the tenth grade at a school somewhere. You do not know where I go to school because I am lying. The administration does not like me because I tell the truth. That is a lie.

I tape pictures to my locker that aren't happy sometimes and if they are happy then they're gay and not the kind of gay that means happy but the kind of gay that means hell. And that kind of gay is sad and not happy. They do not like me because I am evil but at the same time I am God. I am the president and the secretary and the member of a billion things and I support them at the same time I want to take them down.

Someone once told me that revolution comes from the inside and I did not want to believe them but I think it's true. It has to be true. And so I am trying to play their game and learn their rules and speak their language so I can get what I want but by doing this I am losing myself and I do not know who I am or what I want.

My name is Zoe Trope and I am fifteen years old. I am stupid. Am I a writer? Am I beautiful? Is this my fault? Is everything my fault? Did I make this happen?

I can answer all of my questions. I know the answer to every question because every question is a lie and the answers are the truths. But I don't know the answers. I just wanna read *People* magazine and watch CNN and I don't want to be angry anymore. I am Zoe Trope I am Zoe I am being diplomatic and I never say what I think or feel. I am Zoe Trope I am Zoe. Do you know who I am? Where am I? This is all a lie. I do not tell the truth. These are lies. Do not believe me I am Zoe/Zoe Trope.

3.26
Day one. Approximately 10 P.M.

Maybe it's more like day negative one. Or day zero. I'm sitting on a lumpy mattress in a cheesy Motel 6 in Medford, listening to Tori (and my father on the telephone) and thinking too much and feeling too tired.

Morning began with oatmeal and orange juice in front of my computer. The phone rings—it's Thea—and the doorbell rings—it's Scully—and somehow I manage to answer both at the same time.

My dyke fantasy spends hours with me in bed, pushing all of the sheets and blankets to the floor. I laugh and find more CDs to spin in my blue boom box. Her polaroid camera is dangerous and I think of a Thea Hillman parody:

What's the difference between love and kiddie porn?

Kiddie porn is FOREVER.

Scully and I are now forever linked by compromising pictures, ones that will haunt me in my future career as a famous writer.

Between all the kisses, a suitcase and pink backpack are filled with clothes and words and music. She drives north and my father and I drive south and I turn up the sound in my ears so I can't hear anything.

My mother's been kind of weird lately. Tense. Maybe it's because my brother's home and Scully's been around and I'm going to San Fran and her daughter is a writer and her son is a sloth and who knows.

After dropping off Scully on Sunday night, my mother prods gently:

"You're pretty quiet, Zoe. Tired?"

"Yep."

"Don't get smart with me, young lady, I'll beat the dogshit out of you!"

My kind, loving mother threatening to beat something OUT of me that isn't even IN me.

3.27

Day two. 7:01 A.M.

The Oregon/California state line is passed and I expected to feel something as we drove over the line. A twitch, a tingle, a vibration, SOMETHING. Nothing. I felt nothing.

But for you, California, for you, San Francisco, I would fake a State Line Orgasm.

As we approached the agricultural station, my father asked if we had any fruit in the car. "Just me," I said with a smile.

FUN CAR GAME #1: As you pass other motorists on the road, count how many of them are picking their noses. No, really. Nose picking is more prevalent and widespread among long-distance travelers and tourists than you might think.

ADJUSTMENT TO FCG #1: Count the number of nose pickers from each state. So far, Iowa and Nevada are neck and neck with three nose pickers apiece, while Washington has only two. California has taken the lead with six.

NOTE: Sadly, my very own father has become nose picker number two from Oregon. Way to go, Dad.

✦✦

10:29 A.M.

Beatles, "Paperback Writer." Oldies radio station blasting through agricultural fields of northern California.

This is my book tour road trip: doing eighty down the five south, windows rolled down, yelling into the air. I wanna be a paperback writer, paperback writer.

FUN CAR GAME #2: Count logging trucks and note their pro-industry slogans.

AMERICA'S RENEWABLE RESOURCE—TREES!

SO MANY TREES, SO LITTLE TIME

WOOD—NOT JUST FOR GAY PORN STARS ANY-MORE!

TREES—THEY'RE CHEWABLE!

McTREES—BILLIONS AND BILLIONS LOGGED

3.28

The library looks more like a fancy museum, glass walls, reflective surfaces, and staircases. Down into a meeting room, chairs and eyes waiting. My father takes pictures and I am five years old. This is my first school play. I try so hard not to forget my lines.

Business cards placed in my palm and words tossed at my head. Thirteen books sold, my hands move quickly, scribbling my name and pushing $5 into my wallet.

Can I interview you? Here's our press packet. E-mail my editor.

Lesbian Jewish seder on a boathouse. I am surrounded by dykes in ties and my father willingly eats matzoh-ball soup. I try to keep my eyes on my tofu and repeat a mantra in my head: Don't swoon, don't swoon, don't swoon.

These people are too beautiful for me. I am a silly girl with messy red curls and a fortysomething father.

In my dreams, I fuck Winona Ryder. Doe eyes, dark hair, pale skin. This is my first dream about fucking a girl. I think that the queer vibes of Frisco are affecting my brain.

A voice is left on my cell phone. She is rejected from Reed, put on a waiting list. I sigh and think of ways to save her.

3.29

Upside-down cheerleader legs in the window, my book shining behind the glass. Pleated skirt pooled around the waist to reveal lacy underwear. What a display.

White pepper flowers wait for me. "Some girl brought these for you and said, 'Make sure Zoe gets these.'" I breathe them in and try not to sneeze.

Short wiry brown curls, freckled face and arms, butter-fly tattoos curling up her arm, upside-down moon for a mouth with a smile that showcases her pink gums and hard white teeth. Words about being poor in east San Diego and falling in love and counting pennies.

I am such a rock star, I do a cover of Thea's "Dear Mrs. Porter" and I feel like I need a guitar, I need to tune it and tell a joke. Anything to stall, eat up a few more minutes in front of their faces.

She says I am Bukowski, Genet, and Buffy the Vampire Slayer. My cheeks turn red and match my hair. I am called up to the front, a literary show-and-tell. This is what I've got, this is the person who gave it to me. It's special because of the cheerleaders, because it's me. Not everyone thinks that. Some people don't even want to know I have it. Sometimes I have to lie. But *this* is not a lie.

Hand pops into the air and the first thing they want to know is: IS THIS YOUR DAD? More business cards, a college professor invites me to his college. My neck aches from nodding, teeth ache from smiling.

He turns on the tape recorder and I watch the reels spin slowly. This makes me nervous. My sloppy anxious words are permanent. This is the first time my voice has been recorded and I wonder how many times he would listen to it.

Pizza slices and lemonade, we talk over greasy food. I'm sad when we're back on the freeway, heading toward our ghetto motel room in south San Francisco.

3.30
CNN wakes me from lumpy hotel slumber. I groan, roll over. My father prods me out of bed and we stumble out of the hotel into blinding San Francisco sun. DOES IT EVER RAIN HERE?

South on El Camino Real, stop at IHOP for French toast and an orange freeze. My finger traces lines on a map, bitten fingernail pausing over Stanford, Santa Clara, Santa Cruz. Hours and miles later, I'm wandering around these ghost campuses helplessly. They are mostly empty and I feel the same way. A giant wooden cross guards the entrance to Santa Clara. A giant fleshy brain guards the entrance to Stanford. I am not welcome. I am lost. I am a little girl on her book tour and I don't know where I'm going tonight or in two years. I fall asleep in the car between campuses and I don't want to wake up. My father tugs me out of the car to walk around another campus. Hands dig into my pockets. I am homesick.

I want a chocolate-banana milk shake and we are the only white people in Jack in the Box on Telegraph Avenue. Weight shifted nervously and I am angry at my school, my neighborhood, the entire world for being so pale. This shouldn't make me uncomfortable. This shouldn't.

Forgot to explain Tre Arrow, missed reading an entry, and I didn't get a Q&A session. My books sell out, I gather e-mail addresses. Lesbians and guitars and I'm just a little girl with a little book. After the last word hits the floor, we hit the road. I'm driving out of California and my eyes are so heavy. Don't fall asleep, don't fall asleep. My father is snoring, I'm pushing eighty on the five north. I'm leaving my tour behind, going back to Portland, back to school, back to that building with those people who have no idea where I've been or what I've done.

Cell phone ringing in my ear around Salem and I wake up with a snort. Maternal worry, are you okay? We'll be home in forty-five minutes. We pull into the driveway and my slug legs slide out of the car. I'm home. I'm sick. I'm homesick and alone and my mother hugs me tight.

4.1

I wish that I could inherit all of Chuck Palahniuk's great literary skill just by reading his book, that I could become fabulous by osmosis. Or something.

I've actually met him in person before. Kind of. He was at this book-reading event I went to in September and I was so totally in the same room with him and everything. He had stringy brown hair down to his chin and looked nothing like the grinning picture on the inside of his book jacket.

Chuck the Marvelous. Chuck the God. Chuck the Better-than-Me.

Chuck the I-Can-Write-a-Poignant-Novel.

Chuck the I'm-So-Fucking-Brilliant-Brad-Pitt-Stars-in-My-Movies.

Chuck the I Hate You. Because I'm Jealous of You.

4.2

I hate the spring. It's sunny today and I hate the light creeping between the spaces in the blinds. It's almost summer if

I want it to be and she's almost home and I'm almost gone. You didn't really expect me to stay here, did you? I couldn't, not even if I tried. Couldn't watch *Schindler's List* forever and make signs for his locker forever or read books forever.

Anything in motion desires to stay in motion and I've yet to invent a way to deceive physics. Maybe someday, when I get a better costume. When I convince the world that I don't exist. When I slip a mask over my eyes and reinvent myself. But I can't stay here long enough to do that.

◆◆

Your humanity. That's what I really love about you. The humanity I see in you, on you, the things that people hide or try to ignore. The pieces of yourself that you adore and others would reject. You worship what others condemn. You are a temple to yourself and everyone else is ashamed to even admit their religion.

Your humanity. The comic book you carry with you into the bathroom. The way your toes wriggle free from their socks (when most people won't take off their shoes). The hair sprinkled on your legs and blooming in your armpits make you a beatnik bohemian lesbian. I say it's pride. I say it's admission and recognition of a body you won't deny.

You know yourself better than some people will ever know themselves. These people are shoving themselves into boxes and cutting off the circulation to their hearts and smiling like it's the most natural thing in the world. Since when was it natural or right or okay to lie about everything? To lie about the body you're in and the heart in your chest and the lips on your distorted face?

And nobody believes you. Nobody believes the lies we live because we all know the truth. Our truth. The truth is you read when you shit and your hair keeps you warm and when I bite your nipples you suck the air in through your clenched teeth so hard I think there's no air for me to breathe and your handwriting is slightly illegible but so is everybody's.

So is everybody's.

Everybody's heart is beating and everybody's bathroom is dirty and we all have a lot more in common than we think.

And that's what I love about you. Your humanity. You are changing the world and you don't even know it.

4.3

I can run the mile in thirteen minutes and twenty-three seconds but I can't catch up to anyone else or wait for them. And this will never matter. Shocking and revealing, have my heart on a plate.

I can't hit a tennis ball but I can read my paper aloud in English class about queers and make their heads turn.

I can be told for the ONE THOUSANDTH TIME:

"WE CARE ABOUT YOU AND BACKLASH ISN'T

FUN AND WE'RE JUST WORRIED ABOUT WHAT YOU'RE GETTING YOURSELF INTO BECAUSE YOU HAVE NO IDEA WHAT THIS IS LIKE SO BE CAREFUL BE QUIET."

So just be quiet, sweetie. Don't get quoted in the newspaper. Don't start any queer clubs. Don't draw attention to yourself and

Don't. Get. Hurt.

BUT DO YOU KNOW WHAT HURTS? YOU HURT. YOUR ASSUMPTIONS HURT AND HOW DARE YOU REQUEST MY SILENCE.

What will you request next? Lies? "No, Zoe, don't tell them you're gay. They might hurt you."

If you ask me to hide it and be quiet about it, next you'll ask me to change it and not even BE it at all because life will be easier that way.

But what if I'm gay and I have a girlfriend?

What if this offends people?

BUT I AM AND I DO AND IT WILL AND YOU CAN'T CHANGE THAT NO MATTER HOW EASY THINGS MIGHT BE.

And I'm sorry. But I won't lie for you.

4.7

White cheddar popcorn, hershey's kisses, raspberry sorbet, chocolate cream double-stuff oreos, fresca, and licorice.

Habit, repetition, boredom? Does any of that actually taste like what I think it is?

I can't giggle and flip my hair and say, "Oh, well, I'll just have to drink water and starve myself for the next week to drop these two or three pounds!" I can't give myself excuses like that. I'm beyond excuses like that.

I went to a psychologist/therapist a few months ago. I only went once. He made a couple conclusions based on our short conversation: I have "issues" with having a "big" body. Apparently his daughter had a "big" body as well and she was constantly adjusting to it. Or something like that. I'd always thought I was comfortable with my size and weight and body, compared to other girls my age. Listening to girls in the locker room makes me want to throttle each of them one by one. So I was fairly certain his first conclusion was wrong. I'm fat, I'm okay with it, and it doesn't really bother me. It never has bothered me because no one has ever made an issue out of it. My family's always been supportive of me and they've always told me they love me, so it just didn't matter.

His second conclusion was that I had issues with women. He made this conclusion because I had requested to see a male psychologist. Why a male psychologist? Because women, as older-adult-type-authority-figures, tend to bother me. I just don't get along with them very well. This guy made it sound like I had major issues with women and couldn't relate to them at all and something was really wrong.

And now I have a girlfriend and people are telling me I'm heterophobic because I'm afraid of penises because someone must have hurt me in the past.

I don't know. I'm biphobic because of all the negative connotations associated with the label *bisexual* and I'm heterophobic because typical heterosexual relationships make me nauseous and I'm not gay because lesbians don't want to fuck boys and I am lying to everyone all the time.

It's just love. It's just a little four-letter word, it's just whispered between "I" and "you" before you make her come, it's just a heart-shaped symbol, it's just all you need, according to John Lennon.

4.10

"I don't think you're crazy" is always so reassuring, but Tupperware has a habit of whispering it late at night when I'm having a moment of self-loathing and can't stand my hands and my mouth all the words I say. But it doesn't seem to matter.

You're not crazy, you're just not sane and THAT makes you an artist.

Late-night phone calls are my addiction but his voice even more so slipping out of him and into me his voice proclaiming *I love you*

His voice whispering *I know I know I know*

I miss him more than I've ever missed anyone I haven't met yet. I wanna remix everything he says and crawl inside his ear and slam-dance on the multicolored neon glow disco dance floor in his brain. I'd tease my hair out and blow-dry it like Farrah Fawcett, put on a baby t-shirt and tiny racing shorts and roller skates and I would be the roller diva of his heart and mind.

I have been in love with him one million times. Forever is a stupid promise that no one can ever really keep, but we already have. We've already done all of this a thousand times, but we were wearing different costumes and calling each other different names. So forever isn't from now until then, but from then until now. We've kept a backward promise and it's still coming true.

And I have met him but I'm just waiting to meet him again and we're in the same house but he's in a different room and his throat is red and raw from screaming my name across so many thousands of years and miles but I hear him. And I keep hearing him. That little voice in my head moving my lips from time to time.

I feel possessed by him and vice versa. His wrists were broken but I was the notebook on the table and I feel his words all over me. I saved him like he saved me. I was sitting on the windowsill.

His voice changes when he says *I love you*. Everyone's does. Such revered words, like praying to Jesus and murmuring his name.

oh god grant me mercy Ilovehim.

I'm in love with him and I can't stop because I've never stopped.

If I wrote six thousand words a day, I'd just write his name three thousand times.

✦✦

Today is the Day of Silence but so much for silence. I've been forced to speak quite a few times today and I feel like a failure. It makes me think of being little and walking around the house with my eyes closed, arms outstretched, groping at walls and furniture. I'd always run into something, get a bruise. My eyes would fly open and I would be so grateful that I really could see. I was just pretending to be blind.

Maybe today I'm just pretending to be mute. Pretending to be silent. Pretending to be oppressed.

I heard a rumor that some parents were really upset about the Day of Silence and didn't want their kids to go to school today. And the administration is upset because somehow the school was affiliated with the Day of Silence on some website.

Rumors, I hope.

But Case Boy, ever the ignorant schmuck, wrote his own flyer and stapled it to his shirt. It basically explained what the DOS was supposed to be, then went on to condemn it as a useless form of protest.

SILENCE KEEPS THE SILENT SILENT he wrote in giant black letters on his arm. He just didn't understand how being silent for one day would change anything.

◆◆

Secretly, I worry that everyone will be disappointed with me the second time around. I can't concentrate enough to NOT think of every single person who's ever read my book. I can see their faces and read their e-mails and I know them and these people think they know me.

I'm sorry for going crazy and being fifteen and falling in love for the first time.

My apologies for the backseat makeout sessions. I will try harder, do better, I will not waste away for nine months a year, I will save myself, I will be diplomatic, I will self-censor and swallow my own damn tongue.

I will make firm, accurate decisions about gender and sexuality.

I'm sorry about my slow-witted principal with a twitchy face.

I'm sorry for all the really great lies I've told.

I think I've learned how to lie really well to everyone this year. The only problem is, if you tell lies for too long, you forget how to tell the truth. I forget what the truth is sometimes. I forget what he looks like. He comes up to me and shakes my hand but he's an old friend whose name I can't remember. Truth? What's the truth?

My name is Zoe Trope and I wanna be a professional liar.

4.11

Dodgeball is the lamest sport ever.

It's not even a sport, y'know. I want to sound modern and new and trendy and tell you that high school really has changed a lot since you were there. But no. It hasn't.

We're still playing dodgeball.

The girls still stand in the back, arms folded, chewing gum. And the boys still run up to the front, chucking balls at their friends and enemies.

The phrase "You throw like a girl" flies through the air more often than the foam balls.

I linger in the back, trying to decide if this is worse than kickball. When I can't make up my mind, I deliberately step to the left and feel the stinging sensation of a ball making contact with my shins.

"Zoe's out!"

Yeah, I am.

✦✦

For the one with the sloped forehead and knuckles dragging on the ground.

I just got done with my state test in English. Multiple-choice questions on Faulkner and Frazier and what is he trying to say about contemporary writers and what does *snagged* mean in this selection?

But wait! MY HEART IS NOT A MULTIPLE-CHOICE QUESTION! Oh, you silly girl. Who cares about hearts? Do you have a number-two pencil?

On my student information sheet, I made sure to check that I was in "special education" and "non-English proficient."

No me gusta el examen.

✦✦

A teacher e-mailed me last night. Cryptic two-sentence message asking how the Day of Silence had gone and if anyone had any feedback. I told her about the students and about Case Boy's condemnation of the whole thing. I also asked her if she even thought our school should have a GSA. Even the teacher who supports us the most doesn't seem to really want it to happen. She says she's scared of the backlash, scared of us getting hurt.

Everyone keeps telling us that we're just so much more mature than all the other students and maybe we can handle having a GSA but other kids won't be able to handle it. I say:

"Maybe the men who beat Matthew Shepherd to death just weren't as mature as everyone else."

4.12

She's got holes in her jeans but I think she put them there on purpose. She doesn't look like the type who would do anything rugged enough to get holes in her jeans. It's not like you can rock climb or skateboard in pink plastic flip-flops.

4.13

I play my music in my CD player instead of a turntable and mix CDs are a proclamation of true love (much like mix tapes in the eighties) but really, everything is exactly the same.

To shrink even smaller, I tell myself that everyone falls in love the exact same way and there is NOTHING special about us and how we feel for each other. It's all been done before and it's been done so much better so why do we even bother? Maybe I enjoy remixing the same words and feelings to make them my own. But in the end it's all just feelings and words and pretty metaphors.

Scully doesn't have my heart, she has the heart in my brain, the sloppy valentine from second grade, the chocolate candy, the curve of my index fingers and thumbs touching together to make a hand heart. And I can say it beats for her but that's a lie too. My fifth-grade teacher told us the heartbeat is involuntary, meaning you can't stop it. It just beats on and on and you don't have any control over it. You don't think about it, it just beats.

Sometimes I feel ashamed and stupid for all the times I

laughed at teenage love and now look at me, I'm a glowing example. I am the demonstration. I am the diagram and charts. I'm all the sappy words and sugary feelings and there's NO difference. None. And everyone I ridiculed is throwing tomatoes at ME. Sometimes the boys and girls walking down the hall together holding hands or making out against lockers make me want to scream. But I can't. Because I am just like, just as bad as them.

There is nothing special about falling in love. This is habit, this is routine, this is a learned, natural ability.

4.16

Everyone's afraid that the bad things they do will catch up with them eventually. All that karma will build up and really fuck you over in the end. But I'm not worried about karmic holocaust or damaging myself in much more subtle ways. My greatest fear is becoming the people I never wanted to be.

I don't want to be the Old Man. I don't want to be the Vegan Grrl. I don't want to burn out and lose my soul to make everyone else happy. The Old Man smiles all the time and he laughs but it will never be sincere to me. He's always so stressed. Always. And he believes that nothing will get done unless he does it himself. And Vegan Grrl tried to save all her classmates and got so sick of trying to accomplish anything in a school full of ignorance. I see so much of myself in them and them in me and I hate it. I hate myself for it. I hate my self-righteousness and my stubbornness and my superiority.

I'm sickening.

I didn't have any patience for people last year but I'm absolutely done this year. I wonder why I keep going back there. Why keep going back to a place that makes you feel so utterly defeated? How can one place make people feel so helpless after just two years? So many people I've known gave up after their sophomore years, theoretically when it mattered the most. You have to be the most beautiful before you get out of here but no one cares.

No one cares. Apathy is a disease and some days I long for it. I kiss people who have it with the hope of infection. But I still care. And I care too much. And I don't want to care. Caring gives me headaches and makes me cry and makes me hate myself because don't you people understand that

YOU ARE PEOPLE TOO

And youth is not the ultimate excuse no matter how much you want it to be. No matter how much I want it to be.

I hate to admit my humanity. I just want to ignore it and ignore myself and ignore everything and turn numb like my cold bare toes. It's just a stupid literary magazine in a stupid high school that no one even reads. So why should I create a workshop and buy refreshments and try so hard to help people and make them think?

RULE #478: DON'T TRY TO MAKE PEOPLE THINK. IT'S USELESS.

Why bother. Maybe I should just accept the fact that people are stupid assholes and I'm one of them and I should just get over myself. Get over everything.

Linux Shoe has his art and Poke has his music and Margot has her tiny frame and pouty lips and I get to be empathic and miserable. I get to talk and no one has to listen. And no one can care that I have a full load of classes and work on writing a book and poetry slam competitions and I'm the president of the earth club and I'm trying to start a fucking Gay-Straight Alliance and

Just tell me to shut up. Tell me to stop complaining. Tell me that all of this is a thousand times easier than the real world because it is. Petty high school bullshit is not real life but the petty people in high school go on to lead real lives, don't they?

I want to stop caring. I don't want to be in charge of anything or care about anything. I don't want anyone to like me or think I'm special. I just want to listen to music and write in my notebook and be stupid and young forever. Don't make me grow up. Don't tell me this is the real world. Don't try to prepare me. Just let me flounder and drown. Consider it merciful.

If this is what I have to look forward to in the real world, just end it now. I don't think my heart can take it.

4.18

I aced a test I didn't study for. Not because I'm brilliant, just because I have no morals and I cheated. It's not really a matter of being a good smart kid, you just have to appear that way.

I am the perfect mirage.

Administrators and other shallow adults are prone to judging me by my record on the computer. They type in my ID number and my schedule flashes on the screen, as well as all of my grades.

A A A A A A A B A A A A A A A

Like some sick DNA chain or immeasurable pattern. They croon and smile:

"Wow! You must work so hard!"

And I smile and nod and continue to ignore my homework and sleep in class and ask for answers to tests.

I am shameless.

4.21

I took this with me so I could write in it but I didn't really, just notes scratched in pencil on the sleepless Saturday morning and the bus ride Friday afternoon.

Shuffling and negotiating, just let me leave so I can go and come back. After school we waited and organized the last of the submissions. I bought a sandwich and chocolate milk with money that was not mine and tried not to feel guilty. I have a running list of people who owe me money and I don't really hate them, it's just easier to dislike people who owe you money. The bus ride was rather long and included a lot of face-making at other drivers and passengers. Everyone looks at you differently when you're on the short bus.

You are instantly labeled as retarded, defective, what's wrong with them and where are they taking those poor children?

We used these thoughts to our advantage by licking windows and smacking our foreheads with our own bare palms. Most people smiled weakly and sped up, others were forced to stare straight ahead due to the rush hour traffic.

Retard quickly became a verb and we used it excessively.

"Quick, retard that old geezer in the Porsche with the 'da bils' license plate!"

"Retard the old lady in the blue van!"

"Retard the little kid!"

I kicked off my birkenstocks immediately and squished my toes in the cold sand. The others ran all the way down the beach toward a tunnel.

"DANGER FALLING ROCKS"

I rolled up the legs of my pants, bright white legs glaring in the sun. Water stretched up to my toes, ankles, knees. Creeping up my khakis, water numbing my feet. I grabbed his hand and waded up to my hips, trying to ignore my wet underwear.

Back at the house in different pants we ate dinner (beef tips in gravy prepared by my mother) and poetry written by the shaky hands of teenagers. Linux Shoe recorded the scores given to the pieces and I silently cursed first-grade teachers for showing some of these kids how to write letters on paper. Someone turned on *Indiana Jones*, at which point I went into the other house to read and relax. Wonka Boy and a few others followed. A girl asked for a tube of tooth-paste and as I pulled it out of my bag, Wonka Boy asked, "What is that, a razor?" I smirked, told him no, just because he's a cutter doesn't make everything a razor. He laughed, then stopped short like I'd slapped him. He slipped quietly from the room a few minutes later, slinking down the stairs shamefully.

In the pitch-black living room, everyone zippered into sleeping bags, I asked into the darkness if he's okay. She went off, chastising me for being so cruel and demanding I apol-ogize and Jeezus, Zoe, don't tell the whole fucking world.

And I wondered how anyone could expect to keep any-thing a secret if they tattooed it, scarred it onto their bodies. Other girls in the room piped up, invisible voices in the dark, asking me if he's suicidal.

"Just as much as every other teenager on the planet," I answer.

Another girl cheerfully commented how she's glad she "got over" her "suicidal phase" early. Growing up has noth-ing to do with puberty or life experiences, but rather at which point you determine your life has no value. I sighed, because I agreed with her and didn't want to say so. My psychotic-melodrama phase lasted through most of fifth through seventh grades. I got over it, eventually. Sometimes I feel that way about everyone:

GET OVER IT.

Sleep came slowly and not until Go frantically patted my cheek, telling me she loves me, good night. I kissed her anxious fingers and told her the same. She looks so different without her waist-length hair. It's cropped short now, near her chin, a sophisticated haircut that Connie Chung might get. And now I can't tie her hair in knots or French braid it like I used to. She looks more naked somehow. She could hide under her yards of hair but now her eyes and neck and arms are bare. And my hands don't come to her rescue. Rapunzel would have had to find some other way down if she cut off all that hair. And maybe Go will do that too.

4.23

It was a weekend of empty kisses. His cold fish lips pressing lightly against mine in some vague gesture of affection while Go squealed, "Oh! How pretty!" She insists that we have the most beautiful kisses ever and I think she's gullible. I felt nothing and I wanted to but I don't. I want to love him again and I can't. And I don't think I will ever apologize for this or our lies or the dozens of beautiful empty kisses.

It was a cancerous weekend. A small group of students had smoke breaks right in front of the nonsmoking teachers. They smelled so awful. Rotten leather, musty barns, burning manure. Every word they spoke was said to my turned face. It's expensive and it smells horrid.

I fell asleep in Go's lap while watching *The Matrix* and the next morning I woke him up with the softest kiss on the lips (he claimed it was a dream). It feels odd to sleep alone again.

◆◆

My girlfriend turned into my boyfriend and didn't even ask my permission. I was just getting ready to be a dyke when he decided, "Y'know what? Nah."

Now he's taping down his breasts with six-inch ace bandages and looking for a Mr. Softy to put in his jeans. And I love him for who he is and I pretend pronouns don't matter but the truth is I can't keep the story straight. I don't know if he's a boy now and he's still a boy in the past, or if all my memories of her are now memories of him. And if it really makes any difference at all. When I kiss him, he doesn't have a gender. It's just a mouth on mine connected to a body and brain that I love. I'm not worried about the future as much as I'm worried about the past. About keeping my memories real and not sacrificing them to match the present.

I don't think you meant to change my sexuality with the switch of a pronoun but you did. Now I'm the girl with a boyfriend and just when it was getting easy for me to be a lesbian, you turn me straight again. I'm right back where I started. A silly straight girl who hates the labels and just wants a cute girl to fall in love with so she doesn't have to be straight anymore. Maybe I should play the pronoun game too, make myself a "he," follow the trend so I won't have to be straight, I'll be a faggot, something I've always wanted to be. And all of our dreams will come true, the faggot buttfuckers. Anything is better than letting them think I'm like them, that my boyfriend must be on the football team ("No," I'll explain, "he plays for the OTHER team"), he must take me to the prom and fuck me in his car and buy me flowers to apologize for hitting me and he really is a sweet guy when he's not around his friends. Don't plan my white wedding with my high school sweetheart because this is not it. This is not happening.

Yes, I have a boyfriend but it's okay because I'm a boy too.

4.24
Scholastic, snobs, interviews.

On days like today it feels useless to write résumés and covers letters for a practice job interview when Scholastic wants to make me an offer for my book. They'll say to me how much would you like for that heart of yours and I'll smile knowing that my pulsing red heart will be sold next to Clifford the Big Red Dog (a communist puppy, I tell you!), and I'll feel fine when they take all the cocks and cunts and fucks and shits out of me and my book when they make it pro-public-school propaganda and feature me in a commercial for pencils and notebook paper. I feel like a snob but according to Joe Weisberg, 50% of the people in the world are snobs. So Joe, I say, then one of us must be a snob and we decide we're each 50% snob, which makes one whole snob between the two of us. The proverbial ball is rolling and all I'm really concerned with is enough money to buy a new VW bug or other fun car.

4.26

Stripping me naked on a cold sidewalk someone pulls me inside.

Simon & Schuster, HarperCollins, and MTV Books are interested in *PDKTF*. She gives me advice on my writing and my book like it's fiction. She says she wants a "narrative arc" and "character tension" and I want to tell her this is

MY LIFE

Not a novel for her to rearrange but my life and my story and I'm sorry it's not a page-turner best-seller. And you want to make it marketable and I want it to be real. My life on paper and you think it's okay to talk about these people like they don't (I don't) exist but they, I, we do exist and you are holding my forty-four-page life in your hands.

But I'll change it to make you, make them happy. Tell people what they want to hear instead of the truth. I know this lesson. I learned it just this year. I've lost so much of myself in the process so why don't you just go ahead and take the last real piece of me and make that a lie too.

✦✦

Teenagers shouldn't have this. I am too stupid for this. Books are for adults. I wanna go back to the library, the one with the Ramona Quimby statues too tall for my short arms. I don't want to reach her or the shelves high over my head. Leave me on the floor with the picture books, the ones without any words at all.

✦✦

I feel stuck. Zoe Trope has come unstuck in time. She is remembering and having flashbacks and she is slowly but surely going crazy. How do you live with yourself when you are reminded at least once a day:

I AM NOT ME.

I'm not me. I'm some other girl. I am not the girl they

love and no one will want to read anything else I ever write.

You have it or you don't, she says. But what if you lose it? How do you get it back? Buy it at a garage sale? Find it at a thrift store? Look in the lost and found? What if you just lose it and you aren't supposed to find it again? If you love something, let it go.

But I hate myself. So how do I let me go?

✦✦

Am I just your spy? Do you mock me because I'm funny?

I bet I'm hilarious and I bet you laugh because you're too scared to admit that I'm you. The stupid teenage girl. You know everything about me because you know my age and everything I do is so FUNNY because I'm little.

I'm the emotional equivalent of a midget and you laugh at me. The politically correct term is: EMOTION-ALLY CHALLENGED.

What is it about us? Teenagers? Do you just like saying the word? Do we look funny? Baby fat and breasts, cocks we don't have any use for, lipstick on our teeth. We're like pretend people to you and we make you uncomfortable. You laugh because we are you. You pity us because we are you. Just admit it, the girl holding this pen is no different from you.

I've got a heart beating in my chest too and the only difference is I use it.

Is it funny that my passion isn't dead but my peers are? Is it funny that my best friend was raped and the boy who did it still walks through the halls of my school? Is it funny to you that my high school has the highest pregnancy rate and is it funny to you that on the first day of school my teacher told me that one in four of my friends wouldn't graduate?

I'm glad we're so entertaining and so funny to you. I'm glad you can laugh because I think you're too scared to cry.

✦✦

I want to blame anyone but myself. Tonight it's my hands. Too much left-brained thinking with the pen in my right hand and my body is my own scapegoat.

It isn't my fault.

This isn't my fault.

My fingers are guilty and my palms are red and you caught them, look. It's their fault.

I'm not really going crazy.

It's just my hands. My stupid ugly hands. They are disconnected from my mind and they are trying to sabotage me. I don't think anything that I write but it's merely my hands trying to destroy me.

I could cut off my fingers . . . but how would I draw turkeys at Thanksgiving?

4.27

I spent most of my day drinking. Not shots from a glass but water from a green bottle made out of recycled milk jugs. Bent over a desk reading books with ominous titles like *Critical Masses* and *Misplaced Blame* and *The Population Explosion*. And my existence feels even more meaningless than usual. And I doubt I will persuade anyone with this English paper. I eat the month-old candy Skull bought and left here. It's a slow Saturday night.

◆◆

I don't know what I sound like anymore. Scratched notes and dissonant chords.

Everything they loved about my book isn't me anymore. I don't sound like that anymore. But they don't give me any excuses, any chance to explain myself. I reread the things I've written and I know what sounds good and what sounds bad but I don't know how to change anything.

I feel like I'm six years old again, sitting in my mother's lap, trying to find the answer to some stupid problem in a workbook. I get frustrated, scream, rip the pages out.

My mother used to make me calm down and put the pages back in but now no one puts the pages back in or erases all the violent pencil marks I make.

I'm just doing the same thing over and over. Writing the

same thing over and over. Thinking the same thing over and over. I'm an obsessive-compulsive writer. Everything is ritual. The black pen on the right side of the page. The crazy pencil notes on the left side of the page. Nothing is typed.

People can do impressions of other artists, paint a picture like van Gogh, but how do I write like me? How do I write like Zoe Trope? Do I put the pen in a different hand? Do I start a new notebook? Do I type everything instead of writing it longhand? Do I just start crying and not stop?

Anxious like I want to please someone and I can't and I'm getting frantic because I don't know what they want. I'm panicking. I'm turning blue. I don't know how to breathe. My eyes are rolling back in my head. I'm falling on the floor.

I really think I'm going crazy but I don't know if I'm going crazy and no one understands at all what the hell I'm talking about. No one.

The whole point of this mess was to communicate with people and I wanted to make people understand and I wanted them to HEAR ME but I can't even hear me and no one understands and I feel more alone than ever.

I wrote to connect with people and know they're all too far away. Out of reach. Past my fingertips. I did this to myself and no one else forced me to do this. This isn't anyone else's problem but my own. No one can make me write how I want to write.

It's so scary to not be able to run away from yourself. In the dream you can run away from the monster but I can't run away from myself. I can't get out of my own head.

It just keeps repeating over and over: you are not her/you do not sound like her/you are fake/you are a liar

I don't know what to do to make it stop.

HOW DO YOU STOP BEING SOMEONE ELSE

HOW DO YOU START BEING YOURSELF

HOW DID THIS HAPPEN TO ME

I hate every song I listen to. I hate every word I write. I'm not this girl. I'm not anyone. I'm not anyone. I'm not anyone. I'm not even me anymore. I'm not even me. This sounds like the side effects of paxil or ritalin but I'm not even on any medication at all this is just everything that keeps going around and around and around in my head and IT DOESN'T STOP.

Every time I even thinking about writing it starts again. I think about every person who's going to read it.

Just stop, they say. Just don't think about it.

HOW DO I NOT THINK ABOUT IT? PLEASE TELL ME HOW NOT TO THINK ABOUT IT AND I'LL DO IT BECAUSE I DON'T KNOW HOW TO NOT THINK ABOUT IT.

How do I make them stop? Who do I write to? Write to me, he says. I don't know how to write to you. I can't write to just you.

I can't do anything. I can't do anything.

I don't know the names of my friends. I don't know what to call them.

He has his art and his chairs and his paintings and he cuts himself and he takes pictures and she writes meticulous notes with different colored pens and he wears fishnet stockings and she obsesses about a Canadian boyfriend and I stop pretending.

This isn't what I want I am not what I want and I'm sorry I'm sorry don't take it back and don't take it away from me I just don't want to be weak I don't want to be weak I want to be a writer an artist

I don't know how to deal with this.

How do you make it stop how do you make it stop how do I stop it how do I stop everything they say how do I make it stop make it stop make it stop make it stop make it stop make it stop

4.28

Someday someone will probably ask me when I knew I loved him. Maybe it'll be my kid or my best friend or my next lover.

And I'll say I'm not really sure. Maybe I'll give them some sappy response like, "My whole life." Or "Forever." Those words go on Hallmark cards and the insides of wedding rings.

But I think I loved him the night I wrote that letter. When I couldn't sleep. Because I thought about him so much. Because he made my heart hurt. Because I wanted him to want me.

But I knew it was real when we were in Seattle. In some stupid Hot Topic laughing at all the stupid merchandise and, of course, purchasing it. And I watched him open his wallet.

And my picture was in there.

Somehow all the millions of inches between us were completely gone. And I wanted to kiss him. And I wanted to cry.

He didn't put it there on purpose for me to notice it. It wasn't some pretty poem he wrote for me. It wasn't a rose on Valentine's Day.

It was just there. I was just there. I was just a part of his heart.

It was the most real thing I've ever felt.

Ten seconds later he closed up his wallet and shoved it back into his pocket. He didn't see me looking.

And then I'll stop reminiscing and the person I'm telling will wave their hand in front of my face to get rid of my wistful faraway look and they'll smirk and say, "Your shitty school picture in his beat-up wallet let you know that you loved him?"

And I'll nod.

4.30

I saw at least half the school in the halls today.

    None of these kids know what I wrote.

    None of them know my words alone are worth

    more than their stupid cars

    and makeup

    and cologne

    and shoes

    and clothes

    My words on paper and my forty-four-page life are worth more than everything they touch today.

    But they can't swallow my words or wear my heart so it has no value to them.

    I wanna be the girl they knew in high school, the "yeah I had math with her" girl and I want to be their one connection to something famous and meaningful and important.

✦✦

Am I special now? Am I a real girl now? Is this a rite of passage?

    They want my words. Thick and heavy and sweaty wearing a wifebeater and asking for a beer: my words are shameless pigs. I worry sometimes they'll do something to offend people, belch at the dinner table in front of my parents or scratch their nuts before shaking someone's hand.

They aren't very smart, but someone wants them. They're offering a lot of money to have them. Dollars for words and I shrug, sure. Go ahead. They're yours. I didn't need them for anything, anyway.

Today I played tennis with my ex–best friend, a girl I haven't been able to get away from no matter what I do. We made lame attempts at hitting the fuzzy green ball, mostly missing it as it sailed over our heads. When she missed, she would grin and squeal "Oops." When I missed, I would grunt "Fuck" and scowl as I retrieved the ball. We reminisced about fourth grade. She was my best friend forever friend. Two years later she wasn't. Now her sister holds a grudge against me.

More questions tomorrow: how much when do you get the money you're kidding buy me a car I wanna be in the movie.

I guess I asked for all of this, didn't I?

He made me say it *en espanol*: "*HarperCollins quiere comprar mi libro por cien mil*."

C'est vrai.

It's true in every language.

5.1

"You make me feel like a teenager and my mother makes me feel like a teenager and he makes me feel like a teenager and I hate it."

Never have I seen such vehement denial of self, but who else would you expect it from? But you can't get away from who you are, no matter how much you hate it or lie about it or get book deals or wear too much lipstick.

It's study hall in band. They are lying on the floor playing hangman. Two boys are arguing about the characters in a Steinbeck novel. Someone put a blink 182 CD on the giant sound system. Just another morning here on my infested planet.

She's working on questions from a thick textbook. He's asleep with headphones over his ears.

Half the room is mouthing the lyrics to this song. Every five minutes I check my cell phone (set to silent) hoping for a missed phone call. Someone trying to reach me. Someone trying to tell me: THEY WANT YOU! THEY NEED YOU! THEY MUST HAVE YOU NOW AND THEY WILL FLY YOU TO NEW YORK TO PUT YOUR NAME ON THAT PAPER SO THEY CAN GIVE YOU ALL THEIR MONEY BECAUSE YOU ARE THE ONE THEY MUST HAVE!!

Only recently has my addiction to people become so apparent. I crave e-mails and phone messages and a hundred hands trying to reach me at once. I don't know why. Maybe it's just me. Maybe I just want what I can't have and I can't make everyone want me.

The agent called me this morning. Maybe I should call him Mr. Agent or God or something. He said all the words and numbers I already knew and told me we should accept and I said yeah I agree of course yes. What am I supposed to say? "I do"?

Elise Howard from HarperTempest (an imprint of HarperCollins) called. I can't focus on anything. How am I supposed to concentrate on acid-base titrations or Harry Truman when my words are worth more than their school budget? It was scary enough when he decided my forty-four-page life was worth $4.95 but now it's worth even more. It's not just him deciding but people on the other side of the country, three hours in the future.

✦✦

I can't remember the last time we did something special together, just us. Was it dinner at Thai Orchid? Or shopping that one time? Linux Shoe spends weekends watching movies with the art girls, the ones who will graduate in a month and smoke cigarettes by the pack with their pretty perfect lips. I wonder if any of them love him as much as I do.

I am the nagging wife and he would rather drink art and go bowling for nude models. I knew I would lose a little bit of him eventually and I make no struggle to get him back. I just hope he's happy, our beds pushed apart at night.

He has his paintings and his paintbrushes and he's good and he knows it but. Who cares. Let him go. Let her go. I was a high school student and you made me a writer and I don't know how to be both. Everyone else is trying to solve equations to find the solutions of reactions of pH with buffers and I'm making notes, falling asleep, and everything has lost its novelty. It's amazing to you because you aren't here but I'm here every day and everything starts to look the same after a while.

5.2

It's not that I don't want to tell stories or don't think that they should be told but sometimes I need distance to see them and I can't say anything when I'm standing right on top of them, feet on their throats and choking them.

They stole Cherry's art, her heart-art, her art-heart, her dripping oil paintings with legs and bellies and breasts. Naked Freud under her brush and they stole it. They put it in a corner and told her it was inappropriate. Don't leave them dirty pictures near the window where somebody might see.

He's a janitor. Where'd he get his art degree? What place does he have telling her how and what to teach? The people who take out the trash are censoring curriculum.

The paintings are taken to the principal's office for his approval. Voices talk over folded hands and a table and it is decided that there will be a line drawn between obscene and educational and right now it is educational and not obscene and they will try to determine what is appropriate for our age group.

I just want it known for the record that there is no such thing as nudity. If you take off your clothes, you will find more clothes. No one has ever seen a naked body or too much skin or flesh revealed. Sex and nudity are unheard of, especially in art. Thank God for those precious janitors who keep us pure like the trash they sweep off the floor.

5.7

They gave us a standing ovation, a crowd full of fortysome-things jumping to their feet and clapping and whooping.

Ask anyone who performed, and they'll tell you it was crap.

"Did you see how many times she dropped a beat?"

"The drums were never with her hands."

"His drum solo was SO SLOW! We were thirty beats off!"

And that's the point, I guess. They all think we're so goddamn wonderful 'cause we're all wearing the same uniform. We all play the same song for eight minutes without any sheet music to read. Wow. Amazing.

Oh, and we're loud. Whoo.

I guess that's the point, though. People are always so impressed by what they can't do. That's what Tupperware told me about writing. There will always be someone who likes your writing and thinks it's so amazing and so brilliant because they can't do it.

And none of those people can put on a uniform, play an instrument, perform in front of a

bunch of little kids and their parents.

I'm so brilliant and poignant and amazing because I was fourteen then and no one could have done that when they were fourteen and they were all so stupid and wow I'm just so great because they can't do it they can't get back there and they don't want to but even if they did, they couldn't.

It doesn't really matter how amazing you are, but how amazing you seem.

5.10

This week is over, right? You aren't lying to me anymore, right? You have a habit of doing that, y'know.

Waking me up on Tuesday morning and convincing me it's really Friday.

You do it to me all the time. Every day. Every morning. Lazy hand slapping my stupid alarm clock. Radio dial randomly set to the religious 700-club station. I wake up to words like:

KINGDOM and LIGHT and LOVE and SIN

No wonder I'm crazy. No wonder I can't wake up. No wonder I don't know what day it is.

When he was told to reconfigure the server, he probably didn't realize that reconfiguring her server would also delete everything on it.

He probably didn't realize what was on the server. He probably didn't realize that the school's literary magazine was on the server. He probably didn't realize that it had to be to the printer in three days and we were nearly finished.

So, when he clicked "okay" and reconfigured the server and we lost all of our work, he was completely guilt-free.

And when someone told her what he'd done, that it was all gone, she was actually very calm.

Very still.

She parted her thin dry lips, staring straight ahead and murmured, "I want to kill someone."

5.11

So I can yell and scream about the exploitation of youth around the world and children in sweatshops and here I sit sweating at this typing machine, pumping out word after word, dollar after dollar.

The exploitation of youth.

They will buy my words for a hundred thousand dollars and make even more money selling them and my words are worth money but my signature is worth nothing.

My name is worth nothing.

I can't even sign my own name on my contract because I am young. I am a minor. A minor incident. A minor occasion. Something small and unnoticeable. Illegal. Inconsequential. Unimportant.

◆◆

Let's blame the process for the result, okay? It's because of the notebook I write in, the pen I use, the time of day.

It's because I write longhand and I don't type, it's because I think too fast, it's because I'm right-handed.

Because I'm fifteen.

Because I'm a girl.

Because sometimes I sit at a table in a restaurant with four other people who are all twice my age and I hold my own

Fork-stabbing elbow macaroni and chicken.

I wonder if they just think I'm cute. Funny. Weird.

It's because I listen to music while I write, it's the wrong lighting, it's because I think about too many other things.

It's because I don't have my driver's license yet. I spend my Saturdays driving around with my mom, going to library book sales in the conservative white part of town.

It's because all the old ladies with white hair shop at Emporium.

It's because I am my own worst critic. It's because everyone is in love with me. It's because I am young and I am eager to please and I only did this because I wanted his recognition.

It's because I want my own action figure, my own Saturday morning cartoon show, my own lunchbox and pajama set.

It's because I bite my fingernails while I write or don't write, it's because I don't write everything I think it's because I think too much and write too little.

she is always out of reach.

she is always at my fingertips.

the person I want to be doesn't exist.

I can't be her because I'm me.

because my friends give me gifts in folgers coffee cans.

because I was promoted to editor for no reason.

because I do everything.

because I'm stubborn.

because I think I'm ugly.

because the girl I want to be is beautiful all the time and knows it.

because the girl I want to be has thin wrists but still admonishes society for ruining the image of women.

and the girl I want to be writes with her left hand

in her perfect notebook

with her perfect pen

and she never doubts anything she does.

and she would never write something like this.

✦✦

I just wanted to let you know that this is all a rough draft.

We can go back later and fix the grammatical errors, the tense errors, the content errors.

This whole thing is just practice. Pretend. We can erase some of the characters in my life and highlight some of the others. The regrets that I have will be purposeful and lead to an effective and meaningful conclusion.

That whole thing in seventh grade where I wrote nothing but four-stanza poetry will be COMPLETELY omitted. My repeated crushes on boys in sixth grade will be omitted as well, as it has no relevance to the completion of my character.

Watching my friends carve initials into their arms in fifth grade will be slightly revised. Instead of using broken beer bottles on the playground, they will use sharpened hair barrettes.

I will be more reflective. I will be less trite. I will be different. I will always know.

I will recognize and highlight my recurring feelings of lesbianism (see: wanting to touch my friend while watching a movie, wanting to ask to kiss my friend when she stayed the night, brief phase of peeing while standing up, beating up boys on the playground, attraction to tomboy lesbians, taking turns cross-dressing with a best friend while parents were gone, looking forward to kissing girls during games of spin the bottle, being dry-humped by best friend at age six, etc).

This is just a rough draft. This is just a first draft.

By the time you hear the story, it will be something completely different.

It will be completely different.

It will be something you actually want to hear.

And you won't have to listen to me whine about chemistry tests (was the answer really .402 moles?) or the boy who gives the best hugs in the world (his name rhymes with beer) or falling in love.

This is the best game of telephone.

It just gets better every time.

This is just a rough draft. My first draft. Please ignore the errors. Focus on the content. Give suggestions.

5.15

Skull got into Reed. I'm so happy for him. He called my cell phone and left a message, panting exhilarated between the words. Mostly he just yelled, "fuck yeah!" over and over. This must really be a dream. I am not getting a book deal; my boyfriend is not going to college in this town in three months. None of this is happening.

Sometimes I wonder if I deserve it. Or if I asked for it. If there's really any reason behind any of it at all. Maybe it's completely random.

One thousand monkeys at one thousand typewriters and somewhere in the process of writing *Hamlet*, they'd write my life story.

5.16
>this is just a drill
>we are just playing pretend
>in case of fire
>in case of earthquake
>in case of nuclear holocaust
>crawl under your desk
>cover your head
>the security guards will check for compliance
>go out to the parking lot
>open up your car
>blast the radio
>dance while you wait for
>the world to end
>when the bell sounds
>when they wave you back in
>shuffle your feet across the pavement
>squeeze inside
>
>this is just a drill
>we are just playing pretend
>sit down at your desk

this is just a drill
open your notebook
we're just pretending
do problems #8–16
in case of fire
take out a sheet of paper
in case of earthquake
use a pencil
in case of nuclear holocaust
write your name at the top
crawl under your desk
crawl under your desk
wait for the world to end
wait
we're just pretending.

5.17
sad assembly.

maybe they did it
because of her
because it's the day before the prom
because they want to see us cry
or they like to watch
nearly two thousand high
schoolers

sit in silence
it's about pretending to be dead
wearing black clothing
choking back tears
lit candles
and eric clapton's "tears in heaven"
it's about morgues and caskets
and coffins
and explaining the finality of death to immortal
teenagers.

✦✦

Tonight was the first night I wanted and didn't want to do it.

I love performing. I love standing behind the microphone and I love how they all watch me. I love it when they laugh or nod. I love it when I know I'm talking and I know they're listening.

I didn't want to read that. I felt like they didn't want to listen. It's the first time I've ever been in front of an audience and I just wanted to stop. Read something else. Oops, sorry, wrong book. I meant to read this one.

It was the first time I was embarrassed. Ashamed. Bored.

Maybe it was just because I was tired. Because the audience wasn't as responsive. Maybe no one loves me as much anymore.

My books sold out. Compliments fell on my bloodred ears. I enjoyed it. I smiled. I signed my name in black ink.

But tonight was the first night I didn't want to be Zoe Trope.

5.19

Michelle Tea's book is sitting on my bathroom counter, just to the left of my toilet.

Someday I'm going to meet her and shake her hand and she's going to know. She will take one look at me and shriek, "You read my book while you shit!"

And I will turn red. And I will nod. And she will never be friends with me.

As an author, I think it's just a psychic ability we have. We know when you read our books while you're in the bathroom.

We know.

I'm waiting to meet someone who's read my book on the toilet. I know you're out there. I know you turned the pages while digesting your pot roast.

You won't be able to lie about it. You have the mark of the TOILET READERS on your forehead.

Poor Michelle Tea. I'm sorry. Don't take it personally. Consider this a formal apology. This is a sin and you are God and I am hoping you will wipe my soul clean every time I wipe my ass while reading your book.

5.22

Today in English we watched *The Chosen*. I had been awake since 6 A.M. and couldn't take it any longer. Using my blue corduroy bag as a pillow, I put my head down and closed my eyes.

Deep heavy breaths were interrupted by the occasional snort. Hallucinations were had about Jewish boys and matzoh. Am I sleeping at home? No, no, I'm at school. Asleep.

Sleeping . . . at school.

Eyelids pry open, a red mark on my forehead and sore eyeballs.

◆◆

I want to kiss everyone.

I know that isn't healthy and I'm sorry. But it's true.

Thin lips and braces and big teeth and lip gloss and I don't care. I want every person in the kingdom to try on the slipper to see if it will fit. I want to kiss everyone and find the perfect kiss.

I want everyone to love me. That's impossible too and that's okay, I think.

I tap my cheek and tell boys to kiss me. I'm surprised that most of them do without complaint.

"Gimme a kiss right here," I demand, index finger tapping the soft center of my cheek invitingly. And they lean down or in or up and MWAH my face. Willingly.

Some boys refuse. Others kiss their fingers and press them against my face.

Most just shrug and pucker up.

I've had a recurring dream about kissing this boy whose name rhymes with beer. In my dream, he is the best kiss I've ever had. His lips are thick and soft and slow and my entire body feels electric when I touch him.

Beer gives the best hugs ever. Sometimes, when we talk, we stand and hold each other for no reason at all. I press my nose into his hoodie and breathe in deeply. He smells like cats, sweat, and fabric softener. He's very soft and his waist is very ticklish.

I want to ask to kiss him, just as an experiment, to see if my dreams are true. But I'm worried that my dreams aren't true, it's a lie, he's an awful kisser, and I will ruin my dream about him.

I worry that everyone's an awful kisser, no one knows how to love me, no one knows what I want.

So I try to make it easy for them.

"Gimme a kiss."

✦✦

I think I lose most of my patience with the members of my gender in the locker room.

A short blond girl with beautiful hips and breasts

complains of being on a diet, achy muscles from a workout with her personal trainer. She whines loudly, "I'm a white girl with a black girl's ass!"

I hate people who are beautiful and know it and deny it. By default, I hate a lot of girls my age.

They talk about their favorite slim fast flavor. Chocolate is okay, but mocha is awful. And don't even try banana, it will make you sick.

Another girl hasn't shaved her legs in two days. Light stubble creeps up toward her knees and she blushes, vocalizing her desire for some pants. I'm glad I wear black jogging pants so none of them have to see the thick hair on my legs. Not that I would care.

After swimming, all of the freshman girls crowd around the mirrors as they blow-dry their hair. One girl blow-dries her hair wearing only her bra and pants, refusing to put on her shirt. I roll my eyes, making gagging noises as I pass.

Lotion is applied generously over freshly shaved legs and thighs.

Sympathetic remarks are given to girls who accidentally got burned on the tanning bed.

They ask me if I perm my wild curly hair. I shake my head, No.

They complain about the sizing of jeans. Levi's are too small in the thighs, Mudds are too big in the butt. A size two fits her in this brand, but a size six fits her in another.

I am only slightly jealous that, when referring to sizes, they all speak in single digits.

I am sarcastic and vile. They forgive me. They talk about boys and look at me sideways, knowing that I'm different. Queer. I think they pity me. She's just not pretty enough for a real boy.

I return the look, knowing that they're different. I think I pity them. They're just not real enough to be pretty.

◆◆

The dancers from a local sports team came to my school recently for an assembly.

Black spandex, dark red cheeks and mouths, swanky hips, and long blow-dried hair.

"You know what I love?" I ask.

"What?"

"Anorexic waifs who shake their booties for a bunch of athletes who snort cocaine and beat their girlfriends."

They laughed, but I'm not so sure it was really that funny.

5.24

I feel like a silly drag queen in high heels.

I bought some skirts for my trip to San Francisco next week and realized that I have no shoes to go with them. So shoes were bought, including a pair of glamorous gold high-heeled sandals.

I can barely walk in them, but that's not the point. They're fabulous.

It's sunny again today. I can't stand it. It's like it's summer or something. Or it thinks it is. I don't want to do anything. I spend so much of my time doing things I just want to do nothing. I'd rather look outside at the blue sky than stand beneath it.

✦✦

I hate meetings with my principal. With my English teacher. With two counselors and another English teacher.

I say the word *bureaucracy*. My principal thinks he knows me so well. He thinks I think he is a difficult man. He thinks I think he is trying to stop me. He thinks I think he thinks I am just a rebellious girl. He thinks I think he thinks I am an angry girl.

He doesn't know anything.

I sip cold lemon-water as he talks.

I interrupt him frequently to keep the conversation moving like paddling a kayak through jell-o. His face twitches. He says the same things every time we get together to talk. The counselor furrows her brow in pain.

I sip cold lemon-water as she stutters.

They change their minds. They make me the fool. I am the politician. They are politicians. We are politicians.

I sip cold lemon-water as they talk slowly around me and I listen underwater.

I know he doesn't know how much I am losing. I know he doesn't know how much I give.

He thinks we don't think about how difficult it must be for him.

I sip cold lemon-water as he hangs himself on the cross, nails through his palms, another martyred principal.

The counselor says the homophobia in school has decreased significantly.

I sip cold lemon-water as I think of the three times someone has called me gay today.

They are worried about controversy. They are worried about backlash.

I sip cold lemon-water, thinking about their words.

I want them to meet Matthew Shepherd's mother.

I bite into the lemon slice at the bottom of my glass. It burns my lips, my eyes become red and teary. I think he thinks it is because of the lemon. I let him think this.

✦✦

Finally found my bedroom floor today. On the way down I found a pile of letters from her. Signed with her name. In her writing. With doodles and a valentine.

Love, Scully

I knew that I would probably never get another letter signed with that name.

It's so strange. My heart knows that my boifriend is truly genderless, a creature beyond definition, a walking heart with limbs and lips. But my brain stares at her letters and wonders. Will I have to fall in love with a different person all over again? Is this the past?

Is this someone else? What have I gotten myself into?

My stupid, stupid brain. It can wrap itself around all sorts of stupid concepts but it can't recognize a name on paper without trying to lie to my heart.

5.25

Last night I was Matthew Broderick. I was working in some hotel and there were two guests on my floor—Sarah Jessica Parker and some other brunette actress with a very nasal voice.

I tell them both it's dinner time and they smirk, shut their doors on me. Later that night I crawl into Sarah's bathroom and she's waiting for me in the dark. She turns on the shower, then says, "Let's have a little shower," in French and starts taking off my clothes.

I'm Matthew Broderick fucking Sarah Jessica Parker. It's not bad.

✦

Last night I was me. I'm in the audience in some studio and I think I'm watching a taping of *Saturday Night Live*. There are small confetti machines going off in front of the stage, but none of it reaches me. A guy I know from school is there, as well as some of my other friends. When the show is over, he invites me to come up in front of the audience. We decide to fuck. He takes his dick out of his pants and shoves it into me. We fuck clumsily. Before he's done, he fucks another one of my friends, right there in front of everyone.

The next day a friend says to me, "How was it? Fucking him?" I stick out my hand and give her the so-so motion. "Not great," I reply.

5.26

I don't think it has anything to do with the way they look. Slicked-back hair or the bound breasts or geek glasses or spiky hair.

It's the smell that gets to me. The pervasive odor of queers.

It's something like sweat and dirt and I imagine their armpits are packed with mud. It's something like home. It's something dirty and hot and wet.

It makes me want to get inside of them.

They smell real. More tangible than perfumes and lotions. They are bare and open. I want in.

I want to taste them.

All my desires get confused and I know I'm not homesick but I want to go home.

✦✦

I wish you were here with me. I don't want you to be me or to sit here in my place. I want you to sit beside me and see everything I see but I want you to see it differently. And I want you to tell me what you see. I want you to hold it out in front of me and let me touch it. You said we wouldn't talk because your lips would be pressed against mine. At the same time, in different places, if we kiss is it the same? If we both think of it at the same time and close our eyes and move our lips can we kiss so far away? Is it love with the spaces between, all the miles pushing out and the voices pulling in? If we believe the distance over time will bring us together, give us a greater velocity? I wish you were here.

✦✦

I'm sorry we've been together for twenty-three weeks. A divine number of chaos.

I still can't get your name right when you stand next to me.

You are so sexy.

I was so good except when I forgot your name those five times.

I'm sorry. For being high maintenance. For wanting too many kisses. For wanting to hear too much from your quiet crazy lips.

I always want more.

I'm sorry that nothing ever satisfies me.

I feel nomadic.

My arm is sticky against your leather jacket.

I feel stupid with you. Silly girl in her leather birkenstocks and long femme hair.

Next to you, the punk skater in a leather jacket. Boys with tall mohawks stop and ask you about your jacket and I stare stupidly.

I'm sorry for being a high-maintenance bitch.

I'm sorry for wanting so much from so far away.

But maybe the truth is that I am too in love with you the way I am too in love with everyone and I'm just scared. Stupid and young and scared and a million other things I can't get away from because you can't get away from who you are, no matter how much you hate it or lie about it.

I'm so sick of lying. I'm so sick of telling the truth. I want another option.

5.27

We have band rehearsal in the gym. Everyone is marching around, finding their drill spots on the basketball court. For some reason I have to leave to get something and I don't come back for a long time. When I return, the percussion instructor stops everyone, takes out a microphone, and begins chastising me. I just mumble my way through an excuse, not even being able to remember why I am so late. When he is done humiliating me, another instructor comes over to me and orders me to do one hundred crunches as punishment. I do them.

When I'm done, I go to the bathroom. I accidentally go into the guys' bathroom, then remember I'm supposed to go in the other one.

I think to myself, "Jeezus, I'm so tired I'm hallucinating. They shouldn't have punished me for being late."

5.28

I think I am too superstitious. I convince myself that everything is the result of omens and luck.

Eve ran over two birds on Saturday. Someone once told me blackbirds on fences are good omens. I had seen two blackbirds on my fence the day before, so did Eve cancel out my good omens by running over the other two birds? What about the spiders in the shower this morning? Two of them with tiny frantic legs, drowning in droplets of water.

Numbers get to me too. Two spiders, two dead birds, two fence birds. Two and two and two are six, the sum of the digits of my age. Six and six is twelve, the number of months in a year. I try to study the calendar for more clues, but another blackbird lands on the telephone wire outside my window. I count them as they flutter, preparing to fly away. Twelve blackbirds.

✦✦

I still have bug bites from two days ago, small red bumps beneath my skin. I tried to swat them away or squish them, but it was useless. On my back on his front lawn, we were all looking up at the clouds. It was beautiful but I felt stupid. Beautiful and stupid. The two go together so well, matching salt and pepper shakers on my dining room table. They were calling out shapes like exploding tulips and Pokes and my eyes were wide open and I couldn't see anything. It's so strange. Usually I am the one who can't take anything at face value and must find deeper hidden meaning to everything, worrying and assuming while he shrugs it off, unfazed. They saw dogs and kissing lovers. I furrowed my brow, feeling confused, frustrated, and itchy.

✦✦

I feel so disconnected from that building and everyone inside of it. I am not them, I am not a part of everything. I am inside the building but I don't touch anything. I wear plastic gloves and breathe through a white mask over my mouth.

I don't want to get the disease. I don't want to get sick. Touch me. Get in. Let go. Come.

Sometimes I hate the clothing that everyone wears. Everyone looks stretched and pinched and pulled and disgusting and distorted and it makes me dizzy. He shows off his boxers beneath a pair of loosely belted blue jeans, her chubby hips hang out over the edge of her too-tight capri pants. I hate thongs. I hate their toes. I hate their painted toenails and purses. I want to throw up in her hair.

I'm sick of my locker. I'm sick of the idea of being locked up somewhere. Pieces of my life are in a tall box next to everyone else's and I hate it. I don't like opening and closing it, revealing and concealing, trusting and lying all the time every day over and over.

Everyone's locker should be unlocked all the time. They should all be empty. They should all be bare.

I'm sick of meetings. I'm sick of test scores, I'm sick of excelling. I know the only reason why my scores increased this year is because I marked the "Special Ed" box on the front of the form. They thought I was retarded. Maybe I am.

I'm sick of reviewing. I'm sick of covering an entire year's worth of material in two days. I don't like being dizzy. I hate pencils.

I don't like tests. I don't like mathematical formulas that can process and spit out how much I've learned and how good I am.

I don't like the person I was.

I don't want to know the person I'm becoming.

Curry says I hate myself too much and that I should focus on hating other people.

Tupperware says I shouldn't hate anyone.

I live in constant fear of rejection.

I never want to go back there. I never fear rejection because I know I will never be accepted. How can I fear being rejected by the people who will never accept me no matter what I do?

I'm empty empty empty. I want to say they stole it from me. I want to say they tore it from my arms.

But I'll tell you the truth: I gave it to them.

5.29

It must be so easy for you, to be forgiven all the time. It must be so easy for you, to know that, like Jesus, I have unconditional love. It must be so easy for you to write me off. Just another girl. Another opinion.

You don't care. You lie to my face without blinking,

your tongue sliding around your stories so easily. It must be so easy for you to lie to me. It must have been so easy for you to put that cigarette between your lips and light it.

Do you ever even think of me at all anymore? Do you ever read any of your old poetry or stories? Do you ever read anything that you wrote? Or do you deny it like you deny me?

Oh, Linux, baby, I must be stupid for loving you! I must be stupid, dumb, masochistic to kiss your cheeks and smile and ignore the burned charcoal taste on your lips. Lies and cigarettes. They taste sour, bitter, unreal.

They don't taste like you.

I want to be angry with you. I really want to hate you, spit at your feet, slap your face with my palm. I would. Except you aren't miserable. You aren't stupid.

You're just fifteen. You're just reveling in all the stupid shit you can get away with. Your body and your hands and your immortality amaze you. You're amazed with everyone else who is just as amazed. Drunk. Self-absorbed. Fucked-up.

I'm sorry for wasting your time. For falling in love with you. For writing stupid things like this. It must be a waste of your oh-so-precious time.

It must be easy for you to move on. You are a nomad. I understand because I am one too.

I think I loved you so much because you were so beautiful, the kind no one else could see. They couldn't get past your dorky haircut, thick square glasses, pudgy arms and waist. Your short-sleeved checkered shirts and pleated pants. You were such a nerd.

I loved you because everyone thought you were so ugly on the outside but you were so good on the inside. So many people love you now because you are so beautiful on the outside. Your waist narrowed, shoulders broadened, lips curving into a convincing smile. The haircut and new glasses didn't hurt either.

But if your outside is so beautiful now, then what do your insides look like?

5.31

I think it must be painful to teach what he lived. I don't know how he can pull his selective service card out of his wallet. He still carries it with him. He carries everything with him.

We're watching this movie called *Letters Home from Vietnam* and he knows everything about it. He tells us about the daily MIA and KIA counts on TV. The mud and the rain and the way rats would try to bite his face off. His best friends at Khe Sanh. Trench foot. Diarrhea. Communists. Charlie. Grunts. Hueys.

The movie plays a few feet away from his desk and I can see long black hands reaching out, pulling him in, turning him eighteen again, sweating under army fatigues. He stares at the screen over the top of his thick glasses.

I know he's there. I know I can't get him back. I know that no one can.

This school hands little boys to the British Boy on a platter.

"Here, have them, eat them whole, spit out the seeds, spit out their clean bones."

They're going to trial again. Doing it all over again. More testimony. New judge, new lawyer for the British Boy. What will they try to prove this time?

He is contesting everything. His punishment, his life, his hands and the way they touched another boy's body that night.

A part of me wants to confront him, chop him into pieces, put him in a blender set on puree. He would contest me too. The liar dyke who just needs a real man to set her straight.

I tell the Old Man about his crimes. He nods gravely, eyes and face worn with a hundred other problems. He promises to take care of it.

I promise not to vomit or kill the British Boy. But I want to. I want to.

6.4

My thoughts are zombies, my brain is feeding on itself. I think I have that disease he talked about. Maybe if I would just SHUT UP and LISTEN, I could realize that he loves me. I'm not stupid but it feels like it.

I lied. I mouthed the words and tried them on for size: "I lied."

Tupperware asked if I was okay and I smiled all the hurt I felt, I said, "Yeah, I'm fine."

He wasn't chastising me, why would he? But it's the same feeling I get when I walk into the principal's office, after being escorted there by the security guard. My electric body surging with guilt, sparks catching fire and I'm burning to ashes just to prove how calm and cool and collected I can be.

I felt panicked. Why would I panic? What's wrong with me? I should be more positive. What's right with me? I'm just so scared. All my sarcastic comments stripped naked and left in the cold for him to glare at. It's not just him, it's everyone. I don't want anyone to see how ugly I can be and I think he knows. I think he knows everything. I'm afraid he will hate me for it.

Tupperware, hate me for it.

Maybe I just need a shower. Some tea. He will never be upset at me but I'm getting nervous. Nervous and I'm saying stupid things and I'm worrying and telling him too much.

It's okay. It's okay to go. I wouldn't blame you. I promise I would not blame you.

"In the absence of other attractions, nonpolar molecules will dissolve in each other."
—Salvatore Tocci and Claudia Viehland,
Chemistry: Visualizing Matter

6.5

Break. Like a break for a snack? A granola bar, maybe? Some popcorn or juice? A coffee break? I hate caffeine and coffee tastes like sewage, even the good stuff from Seattle's Best.

I think he is Seattle's Best.

But maybe it's a cigarette break. We don't smoke. Maybe those bubblegum cigarettes he bought at the candy store, but no, not really.

Is it a verb? Break like broken? All those toys I got for Christmas that broke before New Year's? Break like broken bones, a shin splint, need a cast, will you sign it with a sharpie? Draw a cat and a house and say I love you and I can show it to all my friends. I can get crutches and limp down the street and show it off to everyone.

Break like breaking up instead of breaking down or what about the brakes in my car, making everything slow down? The brakes that squeak and I remember him reminding me clutch in, brake on.

Break like breakfast? But we're not eating anything, no more scrambled eggs on a nervous stomach, are we really breaking fast? Can you breakslow?

So this is a break. Are we broken? Can anyone fix us? Got any tape? A screwdriver? Superglue? Or is one of those things where they'll say don't fix what isn't broken, like my favorite doll when I was little, she was ugly and dirty and broken but I hugged her tight anyway and is that us? Ugly and dirty and broken but loved anyway? Regardless? Or maybe to us we aren't ugly and dirty and broken at all. We don't see it that way.

Break. Break, brake, SLOW DOWN. Brake, break, breathe. Break, breathe.

6.6

Driver's license and condoms. I guess they go together. Once you can legally drive, you can legally fuck. Or at least now Curry's got a place to fuck but no one to fuck.

"Do you want sex or love?"

"Both," he says.

"In what order?"

He doesn't know. I guess that really makes him a teenage boy, now that he's driving a pickup truck with condom wrappers beneath the seat and nail polish on his toes beneath his fishnet stockings where no one can see them.

I tell him he is going to fall in love and he takes it as a threat or a curse. I'm not sure which.

Hands on the steering wheel, fingers losing grip, he masturbates obsessively.

Skinny white fingers wrapping around his cock and his heart remains untouched. New. Shiny. Clean. If you opened his rib cage it would smell like a new car. There would be an air freshener hanging from his sternum.

He's driving and he doesn't know where he's going but he's going to get there and he's wearing his seat belt and he's got condoms in his pocket. He is sixteen and dangerous.

Shiny. New. Clean.

6.7

I guess this is the part where I delete the silly and awkward pictures off of my hard drive. Her face and eyes and lips are just taking up space. My heart is just taking up space.

Thinking in the wrong pronouns and arguments about genderfucking, oppression, and left-wing conservatism. Our relationship was sour in the end.

The end.

Except this isn't really the end. Nothing stopped, it just dissolved. Melted. We were ice cream that turned into a smoothie that turned into a sticky mess smashed into the carpet.

I'll delete the pictures, but not the words. You can get rid of the images but not the feelings.

❖

Chipped black nail polish on my left hand. He painted it there during lunch on Wednesday. We were sitting in the hallway when he pulled out the bottle, grabbed my hand,

and began meticulously painting only five of my fingernails.

I'm sorry for being fifteen.

Gnats and other small insects pay better attention when listening to tax attorneys and my parents want to talk about my book contract and I want to sit in my room and write.

I don't understand anything they say.

Words are what got me into this mess and words are what I don't understand. Words are what they wanted and now I have to hide them.

You have to send everything you write to your lawyer. For legal purposes. You have to stand naked in front of a screaming crowd with rotten fruit dripping in their palms. For legal purposes.

You wanted me to write everything and you wanted everyone to listen and now I have to shut up. Now I have to spend all summer in my bedroom with my music and my typewriter and I want to pretend I hate this idea but I'm really in love with it.

Hands write words with the same hands that can't sign contracts that touch ears that can listen to the language the hands speak black with nail polish on the tips.

I'm sorry I'm fifteen.

✦✦

I want tears on a telephone but my eyes only water.

"I hate everything!" I proclaim.

After an hour of dead-baby jokes and I love yous, I love everything. I hate it when he does that. I hate how much I love him.

Yesterday, Curry and I went to a temple to pay homage to the Greasy Buddy Holly. Maple Bar was there and gave me her I-told-you-sos about my breakup with Skull.

Curry looks sexy in button-up shirts and I hate him for that. I wonder if he keeps those condoms in his wallet or under his bed. I wonder if I still have the condom Skull gave me.

I remember condom shopping in Seattle and calmly reminding him that he wouldn't need one, since he doesn't have a dick. I think he shrugged me off.

6.8

Train wrecks and plain crashes might be less painful, I don't know if I mean marching five miles or my breakup with Skull. Bitterness exploited over half a turkey sandwich. Maple says she understands. I say, I'm going to start a gift catalog called BIRTHDAY GIFTS FOR YOUR TRANSGENDERED EX-BOYFRIEND. The first page will consist of vibrating squiggle pens in varying shapes and sizes. Toy stores are filled to the brim with phallic plastic and pedophiles' wet dreams. I pick up a neon-green squiggle pen and some extra batteries. He says he likes it, I say Happy seventeenth birthday. What else are you supposed to do for your transgendered ex-boyfriend with a robot obsession and Dance Dance Revolution fetish? I'm a failure. It would have been so much easier to be in love on his birthday.

Afterward I buy a giant orange julius and complain about the way he used to kiss. No matter how awful his kisses were I still miss them. Beggars can't be choosers.

I say Hot Topic spawns bisexuality and no one wants my phone number (except Joe and Tupperware) and other men who are older than me (all of my best friends). They are the only ones I talk to these days, the ones who laugh and ask questions. I tell myself they love me. I tell myself everyone loves me.

Stop apologizing. I'm sorry, I say. Someday I'll learn how to be a bitch. I'll spend more time in California and get a pair of sunglasses.

6.9

Weekends are spent with my parents in the car. Friends call and I snap at them.

"Who was that?" My mother asks.

"She's a dumb bitch," I reply.

"Why?"

"She just is."

I am on the front page of *ArtsWeek* in giant typewriter font. A bigger headline than *Friends*. More loved and adored than Rachel's uterus and Ross's sperm. Phone calls expected and denied. Nothing is quite as lonely as the silent rejection of my telephone.

I think I've spent most of my life on the eye-eighty-four. East and west, pulling me back and forth across this stupid city, magnets on either end. I am neutral. Pull me one way or the other. Tear me in half.

◆◆

I believed that the British Boy had gone away, held back by the rules from the king and the president. He shows up anyway, a slithering snake with shifting eyes. Everyone still loves him so much, they laugh and joke and smile, punching each other's arms and taking up his offers for lunch, a ride home. I wonder how they can be so stupid and easily deceived.

DON'T YOU KNOW HE KILLED A BOY?

And he's going back to court, taking Paul with him, dragging his coattails through seventeenth-century mud. What will the High Judge say, curly powdered wig filled with sweat and stories?

He didn't ask for it. No one ever asks for it. I just want him to die. Please let the British Boy die so I can get some sleep.

6.10

Today I noticed the British Boy is left-handed and I can't

believe I didn't notice before. I feel stupid. Maybe I'm searching for his weaknesses so I can cut off his hands and he will never be able to touch anyone or write ever again. I want to disable him and leave him in the stocks. I want cows and chickens to shit on him. I want the whole town to watch and laugh and know and spit thick globs on his head.

✦✦

I flip through the senior newspaper looking for names I know. They all sound the same, except for one girl. She complains bitterly of the fleshy bodies in the halls, pre-marital groping, and her desire to escape to Brigham Young University, where no one wears shorts and tank tops and everyone has at least six children. They say I'm bitter. So what if I want a people's revolution and mass genocide of teenyboppers, at least I don't accuse my school of being filled with whores. Well, I do, but I'm not so accusing about it. It's just a fact that I state like anything else.

I am Zoe Trope and I am in high school and when I walk down the halls I am surrounded by hookers and whores and I can't even tell the difference and I'm sorry that I don't care. I hope she's happy at BYU, and I hope her husband loves the stretch marks on her belly after six children and I hope there are clothing stores for pilgrims just like her.

Grandpa tells me there is no hope, last semester hit hard. There are no life preservers and the *Titanic* is going down in a plastic kiddie pool. We're supposed to be reviewing for the final and I'm writing instead, smearing black ink all over my hands. Finals. Final what—finally realizing I'm too stupid to be smart? I'm no genius. I can't even turn my homework in on time. I spend more time masturbating than studying and I get off to the same fantasy every time and ace my tests. The teacher doesn't stamp my papers or smile but I never fail because I don't know how. Doggy-paddle in six inches of water, everything smells like piss and I know at least I'm breathing. Everyone else is facedown and screaming, bruising their faces on the bottom. I am lucky. The only difference is I am lucky.

6.11
Something about it makes me so angry. The caps and gowns or the speeches they make or the way the girls wear their caps far back on their heads so their bangs don't get messed up. The gowns hit midshin and I can see all of their shoes. She has strappy beaded sandals and bare shaved legs, he wears shiny black dress shoes and khakis. Did their parents play dress-up or did they choose on their own? Did their parents shove them across the stage or did they go on their own? Why is it okay to do this to us? Year after year,

this class is special because the number is different. I don't believe it. Behind the curtain with my trombone I glare at a person I can't see, a person who doesn't exist. The one who decided it was fair to make us do this, four years of school and then suddenly it's worth celebrating. Airhorns and camera flashes and I thank God I am watching from the side of the stage, that I am behind the curtain and not in front of it. They see the same thing every year. Same group of students and same auditorium filled with parents and same speeches and same caps and gowns and makeup and flowers and hugs. This is the third time I've seen it and I only grow more defiant with each year. NO THIS WILL NOT HAPPEN TO ME. I WILL NOT LET YOU DO THIS TO ME. IT IS NOT OKAY. No means no, doesn't it? No you may not force me across the stage, make me smile and tell you about all the good things and how much I've changed. I peer over the shoulder of my best friend, watching the principal shake hands with each student as they receive their diploma. Do you even know their names? I want to ask. Any of them? Three hundred and twelve names read aloud by teachers who can't pronounce them, parents who can't put a face with the name, peers who suck in their breath waiting for their turn. My lips go numb playing "Pomp and Circumstance." Three hundred and twelve students I'll never see again. Students and parents swarm outside and I can't find a single face I know but they all look the same. Grandma, grandpa, little brother and sister. Mom with a camera, dad shaking hands with his only son. I cling to the only boy I know and tell him congratulations. He hugs back and I know it's the last time. On the bus ride home I look out the window and scream inside my stomach. WHY IS IT OKAY TO DO THIS TO US. WHY IS IT OKAY. WHO MADE IT OKAY TO DO THIS TO US YEAR AFTER YEAR AND WHY IS IT SO FUN TO WATCH AND WHY PUT US IN THESE COSTUMES. WHY IS IT OKAY. WHY IS IT OKAY.

6.12

He says there's a big difference between a B and an A and I sneer, "So tell me, who was it who didn't give you the grade you wanted? Was it high school? College?" The vein in his neck bulges and beads of sweat form on his gigantic glasses. "Don't play mind games with me!" he spits. I roll my eyes. I just wanted a teacher. Was it too much to hope for? Not a vending machine of sarcastic comments or regurgitated worksheets or directions poured out of a blender. I just wanted a teacher. I finish the extra-credit problem, shove it in his face, walk out the door. This is why they call it a final.

6.13

Speeches given to persuade us to keep our legs crossed and mouths shut. Animals and boyfriends are for petting, not eating. He says that gay marriage should be legal and she says no sex until marriage because God will be so proud of you. He asks, what about the queers? When are they supposed to have sex if they can't get married? She gazes at him evenly, parts her tight God-worshiping lips, and replies, "Gay people don't have sex."

6.14

Hours spent adhering paper bracelets to chubby wrists. Unlimited means as many as you want. Yes, you can go on the roller-coaster. I thank God this is not my summer job. The only thing that makes it bearable is Curry and the openly butch dyke standing next to us. When we run out of blue bracelets, she hides the pink ones from the girls and puts them on the boys instead. Curry buys me a giant ice cream cone and I pretend we're in love. A woman with hairy legs and combat boots waggles her brows at me and I swoon. I am easy. I ask Curry to ride on the ferris wheel with me. He says we don't have time. The sun creeps closer to his pale arms. I tug on his sleeve, please, just one ride? He bats me away like the obnoxious toddler that I am.

6.17

I will never understand how washed up I feel on land, how washed up I feel here surrounded by haunting hallucinations of styrofoam and hypodermic needles and those little plastic loops that cling to six-packs of soda. I am on a barge headed out to New Jersey. I am a seagull. I am on a beach filled with hazardous waste. I don't know where I am.

If it's not one hallucination, it's another. I am Princess Leia. Hair pulled up in cinnamon-bun rolls above my ears and Luke Skywalker isn't actually going to save me or fuck me, he's going to be my fag and I will be his big butch dyke and I will protect him. Together we fight off Darth Vader with homo-ray-guns and showtunes.

My most recent hallucination is this: I am a fifteen-year-old girl with a headache. I know a lot of people love me, a few people are in love with me, and I am in love with a few of them. This is normal. I am prone to writing letters and listening to Sleater-Kinney and wearing pink converse shoes. This is also vaguely normal. But then things start to get weird. I am on the cover of *ArtsWeek* in my local Sunday paper. I am meeting my lawyer downtown. I am talking to tax attorneys about earning thousands of dollars in one year. I am drowning under words, under myself, under the speech bubbles that loom ominously over my head. They tell me I am a writer and then send me to driver's ed, where they explain how to turn headlights on and off. They tell me I am so mature and ask me how to change the oil. They tell me I am brilliant and show me where the brake pedal is. I still don't know how to stop.

THANK-YOU LIST

Thank-you lists are bullshit. Every time I read one, I always think: You're the one who wrote it. Screw everyone else.

That's right. Thank you. Screw you.

The entire Future Tense family, for perversion and support.
Kevin S, for inspiring and distorting.
Thea H, for letters that become ritual.
Joe W, for Chinatown posters and love.
Eggers, for curly hair and pirate stores.
Jazz, for 'zines and yougivemesomuchhope.
Mayzie, for Homies, Sunday outings, and love.
Will T, for being my Buddhist and my cheerleader.
Scott the Robot, for the funny cartoons and work sessions.
Stacy, for being my favorite mad scientist.
Strand, for phone calls until dawn.
McK, for snide remarks and trust.
Pat, for being my Holden Caulfield.
Susan, for being the best subversive Canadian.
Kohel, for being my pit bull.
David&Leslie&Nina, for handling the messy bits.

What Came After: A Post-Graduate Thesis

TYPE A QUESTION FOR HELP

Luke types:
I want to hate you

I want to hate you, I really do, but your writing is fucking good, sloppy, but in a good way, like sloppy make-out sessions are good. I guess I can only hope you have a harelip or some terrible affliction, actually, you seem really sweet, and I wish you the best of luck. Jealousy is a fucking bitch. Do you e-mail people you don't know back, I don't suppose you do.

The truth is, Luke, I am a cheap and sassy girl. I don't have a harelip but I've got plenty of other afflictions. I've got accusations of vanity, being self-righteous and self-centered, being an asshole, being a bitch, being a cunt. To which I cock my head and say: Is that so?

Mina types:
you are cool!
thank you for answering my questions, i really appreciated it. i just wanted to let you know that i really liked your book, and my friends find me cool for having a famous

person's e-mail, and to be in communication with you.
they think you are a superstar.

The truth is, Mina, I am not a superstar. Unfortunately, I don't have enough G's to buy a BMW or even a Louis Vuitton coin purse. Shit, the only bling bling I got is from a quarter machine. The shocking reports of a large sum for my writing are true enough, but much of the money has been squandered on petty things—like taxes, agents, and lawyer fees. The rest was spent wisely on necessary items, like textbooks, hookers, and blow. And while I don't drive a Bentley, I do have a very sweet one-speed Schwinn with streamers from the handlebars. Oooh, yeah.

Sandra types:
Hi ZT, I've actually found the original PDKTF and I've ordered it. I loved the memoir . . . just so real . . . it'd be typical of me or anyone to say that you've inspired me to write but that'd be a lie . . . because I'm not a writer . . . but if i was just like everyone else I'd say "Zoe, you inspire me to write."

I'm sorry to intrude but I have a few questions then, about the memoir . . .

1. Scully became your boyfriend, doing so did her name change, I mean . . . other than dressing differently, what else was different? That left me very curious!

2. Whatever happened to "Linux Shoe"?

And off the memoir . . . how old are you now? And what/if any college do you plan on/or are you attending?

Thanks again
~sAnDrA~

The truth is, Sandra, your e-mail makes me want to spill my guts.

Skull abandoned his dream of designing new Gundam Wing models. He's now taking full-time shop credits at a college in Oregon. While we don't speak often, he did take a break from rebuilding carburetors to attend the kick-off event of my tour at Powell's City of Books. He stood in the back, grinning like a fool and blushing madly when I read about him. Later, he had me sign one of the galley copies of my book, which was slightly smudged with oil and grease. It was endearing.

Linux Shoe briefly considered studying the inhabitants

of Latvia upon the dissipation of our obsessive relationship, but decided instead to continue his high school education. By the time you read this (barring any unforeseen disasters), he'll have graduated with the class of 2004, along with Curry, Case Boy, Wonka Boy, Braid Bitch, and the other members of what would have been my graduating class. Linux Shoe plans to attend Cooper Union or the Rhode Island School of Design, while Curry has his hopes set on Sarah Lawrence. To the best of my knowledge, everyone else is headed off to local state schools.

Cherry Bitch moved to Chicago to attend art school and work as a model. Vegan Grrl attends Stanford on a full scholarship where she conducts experiments in lush laboratories. Plum Sweater has spent a great deal of time traveling and learning abroad. Go moved to a different high school after sophomore year. The British Boy was never entirely condemned for his actions, but he's more or less disappeared to college in a different state. Paul Revere said his final words face-to-face with British Boy and appropriately dissolved. Fishsticks and Jar Guard no longer speak to me. The Old Man still works too hard. Greasy Buddy Holly continues to grease and staple and write.

If you imagined a conclusion for anyone, it was probably more or less what happened. Stereotypes are based on some sort of truth, after all.

As for me, I've spent the last six months of my life since

graduation collecting: pieces of paper, photographs, receipts, tubes of lipstick, shoes, bracelets, programs, chapbooks, paperbacks, cell phone numbers, e-mails, letters, postcards, packages, stamps, and tiny pieces of dirt clinging to my tennis shoes. I've traveled to Vancouver, B.C., Juneau, Waikiki, New York City, Philadelphia, and San Francisco. I've been on a cruise ship, a semisubmersible, and multiple airplanes. I ate escargot and crème brûlée. I bought CDs from Amoeba Records and listened to them alone in my hotel room while eating a $26 banana split. I've written a thousand letters, burned a hundred mix CDs, and licked far too many envelopes.

I've been so busy catching up on everything I missed while I was in school. When I told someone that my plans for the day included going out to lunch with a friend, making a trip to the post office, and spending the rest of the afternoon in a cafe, they responded, "Wow, that sounds like a perfect day." I smiled. "Every day is a perfect day." I'm lucky for every day that I stretch my arms, arch my back, and roll out of bed with the knowledge that today, I can do anything I want. The sensation of personal freedom is all too rare. To say that I live a life of privilege is a gross understatement, but that's the only way I can feel: grateful for the privilege.

And this is, undoubtedly, a privilege. Sometime during my tour, maybe on the airplane to New York City, or riding in a limo to my hotel on 53rd, or hugging Stacy, or eating that shitty hot dog on the train to Philadelphia, or reading in front of people that I love, I realized: I am living a dream. Not just *a* dream, but someone's dream. Someone out there wants this so badly they are dreaming of it.

To think that I live something every day that other people ache for, shake and fight for—it makes me shake, too. I tremble in my sleep and try to dream, but it's hard to dream with the knowledge that others dream of being you.

I had a dream that I was best friends with Kelly Osbourne. We hung out in her bedroom, listening to her dad's vinyl collection and eating popsicles. She let me dye her hair purple and we cut up magazines. I found a picture of her in *Bitch* or *Bust* or something and drew a big red heart around her face. She saw what I was doing and blushed, "Stop that."

"Why?"

"You can't dye her hair." She gestured to the photograph. I nodded and later we were on a swing set in her backyard. We held hands and swung together, her purple hair matching purple lipstick matching purple fingernail polish against my white-white skin.

I don't know what Kelly Osbourne sounds like when she sings, but I think that's fair because she's never heard me sing, either.

Dreams stick to you like a skin. When you hang out

with someone in a dream, you think about them for days as though you've already been with them and each moment and activity is just a replay of something already done. I kiss people in dreams and am later shocked to discover that they don't remember our intimate moment, my sweet lips against theirs. We're back to just being friends, being strangers.

Sometimes memories fade so hard that they become dreams. You think you were sleeping while it happened. You weren't entirely conscious. In my anxiety, these dreams that were memories become nightmares of dreams that were once a reality. The awkward conversation intensifies and burns into my skin; I trip and fall in places where I normally walked with grace; I always say the wrong thing; I always sound stupid; and that dress? Is way, way too small.

There's a girl I live with who sits in my chair, snapping bubblegum and rolling her eyes. When I wake up in the morning, she presses her nose against my face and smirks: "Who the fuck do you think you're kidding, really?"

I tell her my dream about Kelly Osbourne. She rolls her eyes. "That's not really a dream. Tell me about your other dreams."

So I tell her, "A lot of my dreams happen in airplanes."
"Why?"
"I like to dream about distance."
We are amused by time zones in the sense that distance

is time, time is money, distance therefore must equal money and how much are we worth? How much would we pay to erase the space that's left between us?

It took seven hours to get two hours ahead: a connection at O'Hare. When we leave Chicago, I have a Samwise Gamgee moment. This is the farthest I've ever been from home. And then we push back, push forward, push the sky out of our way and honestly? I am sleeping through it, breathing warm and heavy through my open mouth, a wad of gum resting under my tongue. I miss my own grand departure, my own farthest step from home.

In another dream, I'm floating down an escalator to the baggage claim when I see a man in a black suit holding a handwritten sign with TROPE scrawled across the page. He leads my father and me to the limousine in the parking lot. There's a girl inside already, dressed in black and leaning against the window, but she doesn't turn when we get in. She doesn't say anything as we cruise through New York freeways. The bottles of water in the cooler are empty. Not that I'm thirsty, not that I've got any need for anything at all. I'm on the other side of the country with scenery whipping past these tinted windows and freeway exits that feel like a slap in the face. No one is picking up their phones. No one. And now that I've finally got something to say, that I've finally displaced some distance, there isn't an ear for my words to crawl inside.

I want to say something to the girl but I'm nervous. When we get to our hotel, she turns to me with a smile and says, "Have fun. And don't try to sing."

I nod and open my mouth to respond but no sounds come out.

New York City in mid-October is wet and warm and crowded. It's past midnight and I'm walking through Times Square, pushing through throngs of people, undoubtedly looking like a dumb tourist with my mouth open and my chin tilted up. All the locals, the natives, they're staring straight ahead. I close my mouth and turn my head down.

I'm eating a ham & egg sandwich at Carnegie Deli and all I can think is: OMG I SAW THIS PLACE ON THE FOOD NETWORK AND HERE I AM EATING IN THE CARNEGIE DELI WHICH WAS ALSO ON THE FOOD NETWORK. I think about going home right then and there. There's really no reason to continue with the rest of the tour: have lunch with Harper people, read in bars, sign books, shop on Fifth Avenue—I should really just go home right now because everything after this sandwich and this deli will be a complete and utter disappointment.

But I stay. I roll over, pull the blanket up to my chin and sigh. I pull long, knotted handkerchiefs from my throat with white gloves on my fingertips.

In the morning, after three hours of sleep (my father snores like a lumberjack, horns honk on the street endlessly, there's a magnetic hum in this city that disapproves of rest and I disapprove of rest and together, we disapprove of rest), I try to check my e-mail with a frustrating and faulty webTV. A journalist in my hometown tells me he went to my high school and interviewed some of my teachers. A kid in some state between here and home read my book and liked it. My publicist gave me her cell phone number for the third time since Wednesday.

Breakfast is $12 for a bottle of juice and two nutrigrain bars. They are the best fucking nutrigrain bars of my life. My father and I walk for miles up and down Fifth Avenue. He takes an obligatory picture of me, hand-on-hip, smirk-on-face, in front of the FAO Schwarz bear. Lunchtime brings us to Ruby Foo's in Times Square and hungry Harper staff. Elise says she went to Northwestern. She laughs when my edamame beans pop from their shells and scatter across the floor. I'm the youngest person at the table, but my father is probably the oldest, and the only one with a Y chromosome. This becomes more obvious when we visit the HarperCollins offices with framed picture book covers on the walls and stacks of hardbacks lining the hallways. People crowd into a conference room for doughnuts and coffee and me, I suppose. No one looks over thirty. There are two boys. They work in design.

One boy with scratchy growth on his face and a too-small black sweatshirt asks me to sign a book for him. For who, I ask. He says quietly, Rob. Behind me, Elise laughs and prods him. "Aren't you going to introduce yourself?"

He blushes and smiles. "I designed your book." Oh-oh-oh, so *you* are the genius boy who I'm obligated to mention every time someone compliments the cover or the sticker or the keen combination of the two. He shrugs nervously, bashfully, sheepishly. I want to punch him in the shoulder and laugh, or wrap him up in a scarf and take him out for coffee. He looks like such a little kid. (It gets better, though, when I read his Friendster.com profile and he includes "humping stop signs" on his list of interests. And this genius boy, working his delicate fingers to delicate bones, is twenty-four years old. The boy who illustrated the cover of my book was twenty-two.)

In dreams, we accept that things never entirely make sense. Sometimes things just happen without any sort of logic. You can fly, go to school naked, forget months of curriculum in a few seconds, and meet celebrities. While we usually accept the circumstances, I have to stop for a moment and question the validity of the situation.

I turn to Elise and ask her why the majority of people who work here appear to be very young, bright, and talented women. She smiles with a shrug: Publishing doesn't pay.

But it should, I think.

I hand the book to Rob, but wish I could kiss it hard

with bright lips or stain his face with my affection. I'm endlessly searching for an adequate way to say thank you. Nothing ever sounds right.

My last step out of the Harper office is a pause. I look over my shoulder at Elise and smile: I promise I'll give you another book. I promise I'll give you another manuscript.

(My heart seizes and sings, briefly, with the hope. I mean it. I hope she knows how much I mean it.)

Tonight I sleep in Brooklyn and dream under a red light. I'm behind a microphone in a short skirt when Jonathan Safran Foer walks in. He leaves when I close my mouth. Tomorrow I give an interview, give a reading, give a handshake to Alison Bechdel, give one last hug to my publicist, and get on a train to Philadelphia.

New York City dissolves behind a long, silver train. Philadelphia breathes. No interviews, town car pick-ups, tight schedules, or brief meetings with important executives. We visit the bell (it's still cracked), walk through parks (filled with statues), and eat at every opportunity.

I read in a bar, behind a microphone, with a paperback that gets softer by the day. My friend Brendan gives me a hip-hop mix CD and Lara gives me books to sign and Liz and Dave and Jackie and everyone else gives me a hug.

I'm in an airport. I'm on a plane. I'm in an airport. I'm on a plane. I'm home.

In dreams, the feeling of falling is common. Your

stomach plummets and you gasp, your eyes opening the moment before impact. You're sticky with sweat and cold with shallow breaths. You remember falling, you remember why you fell, and you remember the sickness in your belly when you realized you couldn't do anything about it.

I plunge down into my fingertips, into my bed. Home. No more bars with strings of Christmas lights, $2 cans of PBR, Daddy buying cocktails, hugging strangers with names I remember from a computer screen, fishnets and flat black shoes, signing my name with a blue sharpie, expensive cars with leather interiors, interviews in Moby's tea house, pink dumplings, or people I love until my heart collapses like a house of cards. I've got a half-empty suit-case, a stack of e-mails, a dirty bathroom, greasy hair, and interview requests.

And the girl. She's still there, in my chair, waiting for me. She smiles and sets down the magazine she's reading.

"How was the trip?" There's a grin on her lips but the sincerity is lacking.

"Too short. Exhausting." I sit on the bed across from her.

"Did you do anything interesting?"

"Gave some readings, drank a cocktail, met a lot of cool people."

"Uh-huh."

"What?"

"Well, you know they were only nice to you because . . ."

"Because what?"

"You're making money for them."

"Shut up."

"Well, it's true. And people *think* you're famous or whatever, so they want to know you. There's nothing genuine in that."

"Shut the fuck up."

"Whatever. You'll see what I mean later, when you're not so interesting anymore."

She picks up the magazine and flips to the quiz. "Wanna find out if your crush is into you?"

Wednesday is a phone interview in the morning, a confused and canceled interview in the afternoon, an excruciatingly long photo shoot for a weekly's cover story, then diner food and wrap-up questions with a probing journalist. I drive him back to the office and get on the freeway home. The space inside my bones is exhausted and weary. My chest hurts and I breathe slowly, drive silently, turn off my stereo. I try calling my friends but no one is picking up the phone. They're doing homework, marching band rehearsal, play practice, sports, something. Despite the hundreds of five-minute relationships I've made in the past two weeks, I am achingly lonely. I want to talk to someone besides a journalist, reporter, publicist, or agent. I want a conversation, not pecking and probing. I want a relationship and not an interrogation.

This is such a small taste—a tablespoon, a baby sip—in contrast to the isolation and fatigue endured by other artists and performers. Pop stars are away from their families for months at a time, performing almost every night for thousands of people, and giving televised interviews after two or three hours of sleep. Slam poets hit the road with a couple of chapbooks, cigarettes, and a rental car and read in coffee houses and bookstores for months on end, too. There's a homesickness to it, and exhaustion, and a desire for normalcy. A desire for permanence. I've got the tiniest bit of this lonely on the tip of my teeth and I'm smacking my tongue, spitting it out, coughing and gagging like I'm fourteen and taking my first hit.

Lonely on tour is a very complicated sort of lonely. It's not the lonely-in-a-crowded-room or lonely-at-a-party or lonely-on-Saturday-night but a lonely that gets down to your blood. It's a lonely that gets caught in your ribs and mixes with your doubt and your anxiety. Healing this particular type of loneliness can take weeks. You have to remember what it feels like to stay in one place. To learn to believe in stability. This dinner is staying, these friends are staying, these movies are real and permanent. You cling to simple realities and junk food. You take showers for days until you wash everything off of your tainted skin.

This particular sort of lonely, an inferior case of the

lonely most artists and performers tolerate, sticks with me for days through cafes and more interviews and more e-mails. I spend a lot of time with my hands jammed deep in my pockets, wearing two or three t-shirts and lots of lipstick. I listen to headphones. I pretend to work on a new project. I sigh and drink gallon after gallon of chai tea.

The girl I live with smokes in bed and reads long novels. She sees I'm looking down and asks what's wrong.

"I'm lonely, I think."

She laughs a clove cloud. "You're joking, right? Fuck lonely. You know half the world. Go have a party." She shakes her head and turns back to her book.

I gather my things and leave.

Four days later I meet a boy who gives me a loose handshake, a sincere smile, and escape. He's got the most boring name I've ever heard. His hair and his shoes and his apartment are boring. I convince myself that I've dreamed him, like everything else, but he pinches me in waking moments. He's got nowhere to go and nothing better to do than be with me, and vice versa.

"You're not dreaming," he says.

"I'm not?"

"Nope. Now let's eat."

I'm not entirely sure what to do sometimes. So I eat cheese fries, play DDR at arcades, go to the movies, pace around bookstores and record shops. I read 'zines, make art, and listen to music. I fill out college applications (Brown, Oberlin, Northwestern, Antioch, Smith, Wesleyan) and prepare to wait for letters in the mail. I attempt to remain ultimately mundane. But there are moments when I remember being thirteen years old and reading *Sarah* by J. T. LeRoy and on the back cover it said he'd started writing when he was sixteen and I thought, God, wouldn't it be neat if that was me? If I had a book with all these flattering quotes on the back and my name in big letters and I wrote for magazines and—

Okay, it was less daydream and more lust, but I wanted it. And now I *have* it. Maybe not "it," really, but something like "it," and something like that kind of feels like "it." Sometimes everything seems entirely ridiculous and leaves me shaking my head, shrugging my shoulders, as if to imply: You want answers? I'm seventeen, you fuck. I'm gonna go cut up Kelly Osbourne pictures and tape them to my ceiling.